Thomas Say Publications in Entomology

Developed in 1991, this series publishes book-length manuscripts on all aspects of entomology. The series is divided into *monographs,* which publishes high-quality taxonomic works; *memoirs,* which publishes works on any nonsystematic topic in entomology; and *proceedings,* which publishes collections of material delivered at symposia sponsored by the Entomological Society of America or other scientific societies.

James S. Ashe   *Editor*
Raymond L. Everngam, Jr.   *Managing Editor*

D0905999

THOMAS SAY PUBLICATIONS IN ENTOMOLOGY: PROCEEDINGS

Steps in Classical Arthropod Biological Control

R. G. Van Driesche
Department of Entomology, University of Massachusetts, Amherst, MA 01003

T. S. Bellows, Jr.
Department of Entomology, University of California, Riverside, CA 92521

Editors

Developed from a symposium entitled "Steps in Classical Biological Control of Arthropods," sponsored by the Northeast Working Group on Applied Biological Control, held in Baltimore, Maryland, on 30 September 1990

Published by the
ENTOMOLOGICAL SOCIETY OF AMERICA
Lanham, Maryland
1993

Contents

Introduction

R. G. Van Driesche

Department of Entomology, University of Massachusetts, Amherst, MA 01003

T. S. Bellows, Jr.

Department of Entomology, University of California, Riverside, CA 92521

Classical biological control of arthropods is the introduction of exotic natural enemies (parasitoids, predators, or pathogens) for the control of either introduced or native pests through the permanent establishment in the new location of the new biological control agents. This approach has been among the most successful forms of insect control, resulting in the permanent reduction of densities of 421 pest species in 517 successful projects in 196 countries or islands (Greathead & Greathead 1992). The method remains modern and pertinent. The need for its use increases yearly as increased commerce and tourism accelerate the rate of invasions of harmful insects around the world.

The ability to apply the method effectively has increased in recent decades because of increased knowledge of natural enemy faunas, increased ability to ship natural enemies quickly between countries and political changes that make natural enemy exchanges possible between more parts of the world. Public demand for the use of biological control in lieu of pesticides has increased steadily in many parts of the world in the last two decades. Training of new scientists in the conduct of classical biological control is important in meeting the social demand for the expanded use of this approach to pest control. The process of conducting biological control consists of a series of steps which are discussed here.

First, appropriate pests with high potential for successful suppression through biological control need to be identified so that existing resources are used efficiently. Barbosa and Segarra-Carmona discuss the factors that are important in the choice of targets against which to initiate arthropod biological control projects. These may be divided into three categories: biological control feasibility, economic feasibility, and institutional and administrative factors. The strengths and weakness of different potential target species need to be compared in some quantitative fashion to allow decisions to be made as to which targets to pursue. A point system for rating prospective species as candidates for biological control is presented by Barbosa and Segarra-Carmona.

Once the pest species have been chosen against which biological control programs are to be developed, effective natural enemies must be located by foreign exploration. Bellows and Legner discuss strategies for choosing promising areas in which to search for new natural enemies. Foreign exploration can be focused either on examining populations of the pest in its homeland or populations of species that are taxonomically close to or are ecological homologs of the pest, in whatever areas these might occur. Bellows and Legner present practical advice on the organization of such trips, including pretrip planning, travel, collection of specimens, processing of material in the field, shipping, and follow-up with the quarantine facility receiving the material.

Once natural enemies of potential value have been found in foreign locations, they must be successfully shipped to a home-based quarantine laboratory where the material can be safely separated from any contaminants and reared for later use. Bellows covers the process of meeting the legal and physical challenges inherent in making such shipments successfully, including importation and export permits, packing and shipping, how to work with quarantine for shipping only the appropriate materials, and to provide adequate documentation.

Once in the quarantine laboratory, proper care for the newly collected material is essential. This demands the active participation of both the collector and the quarantine officer in charge of processing the shipped material. Ertle provides a description of the parts and organization of a quarantine structure and explains its basic manner of operation. Steps that a foreign collector should take to ensure proper coordination with a quarantine facility before, during, and after the exploration trip are discussed so that the collector can better understand the quarantine process and be better prepared to work with a quarantine laboratory.

The culmination of the initial phase of a biological control project occurs when new natural enemies are released and successfully established in the field in the country where the target pest is of concern. Improving the success rate of colonization of new agents is key to making biological control even more effective, because without a high success rate in this step, many valuable natural enemies, collected overseas through extensive human effort and considerable cost, will be lost.

Methods to improve the success of colonization such as initial agent selection; choice and protection of release sites; optimizing the material released in terms of number, quality and stage; and optimizing the release method used are discussed by Van Driesche.

In any given biological control program, this cycle of foreign exploration, shipment, quarantine, and establishment is likely to be repeated many times until effective natural enemies have been colonized and the pest problem is resolved. Efficiency in these processes is essential for the effective use of biological control.

Acknowledgments

We thank the National Biological Control Institute, USDA-APHIS, for financial assistance in the preparation and distribution of these papers.

References Cited

Greathead, D. J. & A. H. Greathead. 1992. Biological control of insect pests by insect parasitoids and predators: the BIOCAT database. Biocontrol News Info. 13(4): 61N–68N.

Criteria for the Selection of Pest Arthropod Species as Candidates for Biological Control

Pedro Barbosa and Alejandro Segarra-Carmona
Department of Entomology, College Park, MD 20742

ABSTRACT
Criteria for ranking potential target pest arthropods to which biological control might be applied are discussed and organized into a numerical rating system. Candidate projects are rated in three separate areas: biological control feasibility, economic assessment, and institutional/administrative assessment. Separate ranking in each of these areas allows economic and political factors influencing a project to be distinguished from biological factors. The use of this index allows pest complexes across numerous crops to be ranked, so that overall biological control priorities for a state or country can be identified in an objective manner and used as a basis for planning long-term programs of biological control implementation.

One of the most critical steps in a biological control program is the selection of the target pest arthropod species against which biological control is actually attempted. In any given state or country there are likely to be many important pests. These, however, will vary greatly with respect to the probability that biological control can provide effective pest suppression. Consequently, criteria that help identify which species are most susceptible to the biological control method are of great value in the planning and execution of broad programs of biological control for pest complexes.

Previous efforts have been made to define criteria for choosing candidates for biological control (USDA–ARS 1984, 1988). To date, however, determining whether any given biological control project is desirable or likely to achieve its goals often has remained more a matter of conjecture than the result of informed, rigorous analysis. The decision-making process used to choose projects has been poorly defined. In the past it has not been uncommon to determine priorities for biological control based solely on the degree of public concern over a particular pest. As a consequence, pests selected for the application of biological control often have been species that are neither those most susceptible to the method nor the ones posing the most urgent pest problems (Harris 1984).

The motivation for setting priorities among potential targets for biological control stems from the fact that financial resources for the initiation of new projects are, and will likely continue to be, limited. Individuals or agencies proposing to initiate biological control efforts will invariably be asked, "If you had money for only one (or two) target pest(s), which would you pick and why?" Thus, it is important that those concerned with planning for the future applications of biological control be able to set priorities in a rational, quantifiable fashion. The use of an organized system for setting biological control priorities would help reduce haphazardness, enhance the credibility of biological control, and provide a clear rationale for the initiation of biological control against a specific pest.

Many factors exist which might be taken into consideration when setting priorities among biological control candidate species (List 1). The criteria currently used by biological control practitioners do not have any obvious characteristics in common which set them apart from other criteria that have been proposed over the years but have not been adopted. Rather, the current choice of criteria reflects the preference of biological control practitioners and is reinforced by past successes. Furthermore, many of the existing criteria among those that have been adopted and those that have been ignored by practitioners have been proposed as the result of the misapplication of current ecological theories (e.g., criteria based on the relationship between species diversity and ecosystem stability) or as the result of the application of potentially inappropriate theories (e.g., criteria based on population dynamics theory developed for non-agroecosystem species). Few criteria, if any, have been subject to rigorous empirical or experimental evaluation.

In this article, we discuss the criteria most frequently used or proposed for the selection of candidate pest species for classical biological control. We propose a new set of criteria in the form of a numerical index for the selection of candidate target species for biological control. These criteria also have application for projects of augmentative biological control as well.

Examples of criteria that have been proposed or used in the past in the selection of biological control targets are given in List 1. A consensus has developed among biological control researchers and practitioners regarding the usefulness of many of these criteria, although as noted

List 1. Examples of criteria used and proposed for selection of candidates for biological control

1. Introduced pests
2. Indirect pests
3. Key pests
4. Perennial crop pests
5. Recently introduced versus multigeneration post-introduction pest (?)
6. Pests of persistent, stable and diverse crop systems
7. R strategists versus k strategists (?)
8. Pests of importance because of:
   A. Direct value of crop
   B. Degree of pest contact with public (allergenic plant or insect versus crop versus aesthetic pest)
   C. Political influence of affected constituency
9. Other methods have failed or are too costly
10. Current controls require excessive use of pesticides
11. Pest is a taxonomically distinct unit
12. Low pest populations (following control) are acceptable
13. Anticipated costs for implementation of biological program low relative to current control costs
14. Availability of infrastructure and personnel to:
   A. Search for candidates of selected pest
   B. Release biological control agents
   C. Evaluate establishment success
15. Availability of economic injury levels and economic thresholds
16. Pest is a long-term problem and is more than a localized pest
17. Relevant information available on natural enemies of a given pest
18. Compatibility with:
   A. Other biological and biologically based controls
   B. Genetically released animals and plants
   C. Environmental safety

?, Examples of criteria for which little or no consensus has been achieved as to their value as predictors of appropriate candidates.

above, the consensus is not based on proof but on apparent success (i.e., based on *a posteriori* analyses of successful biological programs). Examples of this consensus of support for certain criteria are the preferences given to pests in perennial agroecosystems, those that are not plant disease vectors, and those that do not have a very low economic injury level in the crop. With respect to other criteria, such as whether a target species is an r strategist or a k strategist, no consensus has been developed and the favored option varies among practitioners.

What is obvious from the criteria in Table 1 is that only some criteria concern biological or ecological factors. Other key criteria fall in two additional categories; i.e., economic and institutional/ administra-

Table 1. Evaluation index for setting priorities among potential candidate pests for which no biological control programs exist in the state

Biological Control Feasibility

1. Pest origin and recency of introduction.
   a. Introduced.   [1]
   b. Native.   [0]
2. Crop habitat stability.
   a. Perennial.   [1]
   c. Annual.   [0]
3. Pest feeding habits.
   a. Exposed habit.   [1]
   b. Concealed habit.   [0]
4. Preintroduction studies: natural enemies present
   in area of pest origin.
   a. Taxonomic identity of natural enemies known.   [2]
   b. Some knowledge of natural enemies present.   [1]
   c. No surveys have been conducted.   [0]
5. Preintroduction studies: natural enemy impact.
   a. Life table studies available.   [2]
   b. Some data available on mortality caused by natural enemies.   [1]
   c. No mortality data available.   [0]
6. Status of biological control projects on pest in other areas.
   a. Active.   [2]
   b. Inactive.   [1]
   c. Nonexistent.   [0]
7. Level of accomplishment of out-of-state biological
   control programs.
   a. Sustained suppression phase.   [4]
   b. Colonization and impact assessment.   [3]
   c. Importation, rearing, and testing.   [2]
   d. Foreign exploration phase.   [1]
   e. No biological control program exists.   [0]
8. Availability of biological control agents.
   a. Instate/commercial source.   [3]
   b. Source in United States.   [2]
   c. Foreign sources.   [1]
   d. No known source.   [0]

Economic Assessment

A. Crop importance.
   1. Current importance- total cash receipts.
      a. Among top commodities.   [2]
      b. Lesser commodity.   [0]
B. Pest importance.
   1. Consistency of pest problem.
      a. Most years.   [2]
      b. Some years.   [1]
      c. Rare.   [0]

Table 1. (Continued)

2. Severity of damage per pest individual under current practices.
    a. Light.   [2]
    b. Moderate.   [1]
    c. Severe.   [0]
3. Revenue loss by pest under no control practices.
    a. Low.   [2]
    b. Moderate.   [1]
    c. High.   [0]
4. Pest status in crop.
    a. Sole key pest.   [2]
    b. No key pests on crop.   [1]
    c. Other key pests exist.   [0]
5a. Type of pest (not applicable for landscape pests).
    a. Indirect pest.   [2]
    b. Direct/indirect pest.   [1]
    c. Direct pest.   [0]
5b. Type of pest (for landscape pests only).
    a. Low aesthetic damage.   [2]
    b. Intermediate aesthetic damage.   [1]
    c. High aesthetic damage.   [0]
6. Is chemical control cost effective?
    a. No.   [1]
    b. Yes.   [0]
C. Cost/duration/feasibility (increasing cost).
    1. Cost of implementation and complexity.
        a. redistribution and inoculation.   [3]
        b. Importation/research and development.   [2]
        c. Augmentative/inundative releases.[a]   [1]
        d. No information available.   [0]

Institutional/Administrative Assessment

A. State/institutional resource base.
    1. Resident staff with expertise in pest.
        a. Yes.   [1]
        b. No.   [0]
    2. Ongoing research on the pest or related pests.
        a. Yes.   [1]
        b. No.   [0]
    3. Existence of rearing and quarantine facilities.
        a. Yes.   [1]
        b. No.   [0]
    4. Existence of pest monitoring programs.
        a. Yes.   [1]
        b. No.   [0]
    5. Existence of collaboration agreements with federal, state, and/or local agencies.
        a. Yes.   [1]
        b. No.   [0]

Table 1. Continued on Page 10

Table 1. (Continued)

6. Length of institutional commitment needed for biological control.	
a. Short term (1-3 yr).	[2]
b. Medium term (3-5 yr).	[1]
c. Long term (> 5 yr).	[0]
B. Desirability of alternative control methods.	
1. Is the recommended chemical control agent:	
a. Restricted with recent cancellations.	[2]
b. Restricted with no cancellations.	[1]
c. Not restricted.	[0]
2. Is prevalent chemical control agent a potential ground-water contaminant?	
a. Yes.	[1]
b. No.	[0]
3. Are there other biological control projects currently active in the crop?	
a. Yes.	[1]
b. No.	[0]
4. Is there any IPM program currently active in the crop?	
a. Yes.	[1]
b. No.	[0]
5. Is the pest currently of public concern?	
a. Yes.	[1]
b. No.	[0]

[a]When biological control agent is commercially available, treat as redistribution/inoculation project.

tive. Economic factors reflect the relative costs of instituting biological control compared with alternative approaches, or the economic losses caused by the pest. Institutional constraints may involve the level of public alarm about either the pest or the current use of chemical control. Alternatively, the availability of institutional infrastructure may make collection of natural enemies of a given pest, in its area of origin, easier than for other pest species. Conversely, the collection of natural enemies of pests from certain areas may be impossible because of the lack of facilities or collaborators. Although not always incompatible, sometimes these differing categories of criteria suggest different priorities. Our index is structured so that similar criteria are grouped, allowing the significance of each of these areas (biological control feasibility, economic assessment, and institutional/administration assessment) to be seen separately within an overall ranking that is given to the potential target species. Thus, the final priority assigned to any particular biological control target species by our system will represent a clearly articulated balance of biological, economic, and institutional factors.

Nature and Structure of Selection Index

Our index is based on a point system and has three categories: (1) biological control feasibility, (2) economic assessment and (3) institutional/administrative assessment. Obviously, many factors might be included in each of these categories, but for practicality we have limited the number used. The index is intended primarily for use in classical biological control projects (importation of new species of natural enemies), but it may also be applied to augmentative biological control. Because the absolute maximum scores for each of the three categories differ, absolute scores must be converted to relative scores (percentage of total points possible in category) before comparisons are made across categories.

In each category, questions are posed to uncover the strengths and weaknesses of the project (Table 1). The number of questions asked, their content, and the relative point value of each answer are designed to allow sufficient flexibility to accommodate programs with differing goals. Conceptually, our method resembles, in part, approaches used by earlier biological control practitioners. It differs, however, in being a formalized process in which biological, economic, and institutional factors are explicitly identified, evaluated, and balanced against each other. In the past, these steps also occurred but in an intuitive, less visible fashion. Furthermore, our method lends itself not only to evaluating individual species as potential biological control targets but also to applying the process to entire sets of pests in regions so that optimum targets can be identified from among whole pest complexes across multiple crops in a state or country (e.g., Van Driesche & Carey 1987, & McClay 1989).

Judgments as to the relative weights that should be assigned to biological versus economic or institutional factors may differ considerably when made by personnel from universities, state departments of agriculture or environmental protection, industry, or federal agencies. Procedures for setting priorities in the selection of target species for biological control should take these differences, along with resources and goals, into consideration. The information needed to identify promising biological control programs may differ substantially, depending on the goals of each group or agency. Similarly, regional, national, and international institutions have their own goals and thus may weigh criteria differently or incorporate additional criteria. Without a clear statement of a program's rationale and objectives it is difficult, if not impossible, to define reasonable criteria that would indicate probable success, and it would thus also be very difficult to effectively evaluate a program's success or failure if goals were never explicitly stated. The use of our index forces the elaboration of objectives as part of the candidate selection process.

Finally, the index proposed in this paper is intended only for use in setting priorities among arthropod pests rather than for weeds or plant pathogens. We believe that attempting to develop an index to set priorities for all types of pests would be impractical. Although development of indices for setting priorities among biological control projects for weeds and plant pathogens would be useful, we view these as separate exercises that might benefit from the experiences gained from the use of the arthropod index. Indeed, some schemes already have been developed for weeds (USDA–ARS 1984, McClay 1989).

Biological Control Feasibility

Factors considered by our index (Table 1) in this category provide information on: (1) the nature of the pest and the release site (questions 1, 2, and 3); (2) the existence, availability and effectiveness of biological control agents of the pest (questions 4 and 5); and (3) the current status of biological control projects against the candidate pest (questions 6, 7, and 8). Obviously, a large number of issues potentially could be addressed with respect to assessing biological control feasibility, not all of which are incorporated in our index. Readers interested in these issues are referred to the publications of Lloyd (1960), Turnbull & Chant (1961), Watt (1965), Bennett (1974), Van Emden & Williams (1974), Ehler & Miller (1978), Hall & Ehler (1979), Carl (1982), Ehler & Andres (1983), Greathead & Waage (1983), Hokkanen (1985), Hoy (1985), Cock (1986), Greathead (1986), Van Emden (1989), and Waage (1989). The potential scores for this component range from 0 to 16. The higher the score, the more suitable the candidate species is considered to be for biological control. It should be noted that some of these criteria (i.e., those concerning lack of knowledge) will assign lower scores to newly introduced pests. This does not mean that these pests have an intrinsically lowered probability of success biologically, only that more effort and time may be needed to achieve success compared with projects in which considerable information about the pest and its natural enemies already exists.

Some factors usually considered to be biological in nature have been incorporated in our index into the economic assessment category because their importance is more easily measured in economic terms. Examples include the issues of whether a species is a direct or indirect pest, the severity of the damage it causes, and how long it persists as a pest. Other factors that could have been included in the biological control feasibility category were not considered because we viewed them as relative phenomena which are difficult to quantify. For example, whether a pest is r or k selected (Force 1974, Southwood 1977) or exhibits moderate to low fecundity or low mobility (Greathead & Waage 1983) may be biologically important, but the conclusion drawn from any comparison depends too specifically on exactly which life history parameters are chosen for the comparison and under what conditions comparisons are made. For example, whether a candidate pest is deemed to have low or high mobility depends upon to which other species it is compared. Finally, a third set of potentially important traits were not included in our index because we viewed them as impractical or unrealistic. For example, although it may be important to pick specialist over generalist natural enemies or to select one type of biological control agent over another (e.g., parasitoids over predators or pathogens) the reality of foreign exploration does not allow for the luxury of excluding or discarding collected biological control agents. Nor are the historical data on these types of generalizations so compelling as to mandate ignoring any biological control agent that is readily available.

Economic Assessment

A primary consideration in the decision to initiate a biological control project is often the degree of economic loss caused by a pest or the cost of its control using currently available methods. The economic assessment category focuses on information on crop and pest importance as well as on the cost and feasibility of available biological control options. Ultimately, a project's success or failure must be evaluated in economic terms. Indeed, Reichelderfer (1981) asserts that the ultimate criterion for the success of a biological control project is that it is economically feasible only if its monetary return is greater or equal to that realized from alternative forms of control or no control.

Assessing the benefits and estimating the costs of biological control projects have increasingly become paramount considerations. Several factors affecting the economic feasibility of biological control have been identified by researchers and economists (Tisdell 1990). Huffaker et al. (1976) estimated benefits of biological control as the sum of the value of production saved and the savings achieved by its use over alternative pest control actions. An example of the latter is presented by Ervin et al. (1983) in their cost analysis of the biological control program against the Comstock mealybug, *Pseudococcus comstocki* (Kuwana), in California. Their comparison of biological control expenditures and eradication program costs indicated substantial financial benefits favoring biological control.

Program costs have often been considered important factors affecting the implementation of biological control programs. Harris (1979) did not consider any biological control project for weeds in Canada to be justified if the return on investment for the project was less than the economic losses caused by the weed. With a typical return on investment of 10% for biological control of weeds programs and an average of 18-20 scientist-years, it was not worth mounting a biological control program in 1976 for any weed that did not cause more than $150,000 (Canadian) worth of damage per year.

The use of cost/benefit analyses in biological control is a systematic way to determine if its adoption will result in higher or lower profits (Headley 1985). Using this approach, Reichelderfer (1981) argues that the benefits of a biological control project are a function of the type and severity of the damage caused by a pest, the efficiency of the biological control agent, the market price for the crop, and risk aversion of producers. The costs of biological control are determined by the price of the biological control agent and the cost associated in using it. Others have presented a similar strategy, based on crop importance, pest importance, program cost, and cost/benefit comparisons with other projects (Waterhouse & Norris 1987). The economic assessment we offer in our index is based on these concepts.

Our economic assessment consists of questions in three main areas of evaluation: crop importance, pest importance, and project cost. Scores for this component can range from 0 to 18. Crop importance can be determined from any available assessment of the revenues generated by a crop or commodity group. Crop revenue information can often be obtained from state agencies; e.g., Maryland Department of Agriculture (1989, 1990) for agricultural crops, Maryland Horticulture Survey (Gill 1989) and U.S. Department of Commerce (1987) for horticultural crops. Alternative sources of such information also include interviews with industry experts or agricultural economists. When figures on revenues generated are unavailable, other measures of value can be used. Examples of other criteria of value include acres planted, acres harvested, dollars per production acre, or value of total production. The first three measures are straightforward for most field, fruit, and vegetable crops but are inadequate for horticultural commodities. Because revenues from horticultural commodities in some states may be significant (e.g., in Maryland they represent 12.7% of all agricultural production and 36.5% of crop revenue), a more flexible measure is needed to accommodate all types of commodities. To avoid this difficulty, a general question was included to reflect the crop's importance (i.e., whether the pest attacks one or more of the top five crop species within a given commodity group). Other factors we omitted but might be considered important are production trends such as increases or decreases in crop price, acreage, or total production over time, especially if these are being affected by the presence of the pest in a region.

Information on the importance of pests affecting a commodity group can be obtained from interviews with crop protection specialists and practitioners. Specialists can be presented with a list of potential target pests and asked to rank each pest by severity, frequency of the problem, and perceived need to treat when the pest is detected. A consensus of these opinions can be used to complete the economic assessment section of our index. Additional information may be obtained from Cooperative Extension Service bulletins, leaflets, and other published information sources. Other measures of pest importance can include any determinants of persistence and severity of pest problems under current practices, revenue losses when the pest is not controlled, pest status, type of pest, and cost effectiveness of other control methods (such as chemical control). The goal of obtaining this information is to obtain a dynamic picture of the economic importance of the pest, thereby minimizing the risk of failure of the biological control project. Risk aversion is a common motivating force in the selection of pest control options by farmers (Reichelderfer 1981) and perhaps should be no less important for the biological control planner or practitioner. Based on that premise, we selected key questions for the index which have been posed in papers by Reichelderfer (1981) and Cock (1986). Brief explanations of their usefulness for the assessment of risk avoidance follows.

Consistency of the Pest Problem. The frequency with which a pest problem occurs greatly influences the need for treatment and provides insights into the relative effectiveness of natural enemies. A pest with a pattern of sparsely located and infrequent outbreaks (e.g., many forest Lepidoptera) should be considered a poor target (other things being equal) because it would be economically wiser to take actions only when and where the problem arises, and this precludes a sustained effort. In addition, the fact that the pest is not frequently a problem indicates, in all likelihood, that natural control is at work keeping pest populations below damaging levels most of the time. For such pests, alternative management methods such as chemical control may be used to treat sporadic outbreaks. On the other hand, populations that continuously occur at outbreak levels indicate poor natural control and thus an enhanced need to use biological control.

Severity of Pest Damage Under Current Practices. As potential losses per pest individual increase, the less likely it is for biological control to be an effective pest suppression alternative. This is especially true in classical biological control where natural enemies often reduce pest populations but only to some new, lower equilibrium level. For pests with very low economic injury levels, even substantial pest population reductions by natural enemies may not be sufficient to prevent economic damage to the crop. Pests that cause moderate or low levels of damage per individual are associated with high economic injury levels and require lower control inputs. These pests may be targeted for biological control with high economic benefit (Reichelderfer 1981).

Revenue Loss Under No Treatment Conditions. This is an additional measurement of risk to farmers. It is an extremely important measure which indicates the farmer's level of concern about the pest; i.e., how much risk the farmer is willing to take when confronted with the pest. Pests that are perceived by the producer as tolerable, even at high population levels, are therefore excellent candidates for biological control because of the propensity of farmers to postpone or suspend chemical treatments.

Pest Status in the Crop. Very often crops are attacked simultaneously by a large variety of pests. Most pests are usually not of immediate concern to the farmer, either because their populations are generally low or because they can be tolerated. However, some are key pests for which farmers have little tolerance. From a biological control point of view, the establishment of beneficial species to control one pest is usually contingent on a largely pesticide-free environment in which to develop and reproduce. When a crop has only one key pest and at most a few secondary pests, beneficials usually can be used against the key pest with little interference from pesticide use. However, when more than one key pest exists in a crop, especially if they belong to different taxa (i.e., orders), it makes little sense to use beneficials for one pest and chemical control for the other because these approaches are incompatible in most cases. Thus, biological control is preempted, becoming an economically unwise tactic when a single chemical is effective in controlling both pests.

Type of Pest. Insect pests may be categorized in two groups according to their effect on crop yield and quality: those species that consume plant (or animal) parts of no commercial value are termed "indirect pests," whereas those that damage the desired product are referred to as "direct pests." However, these categories typically are neither steadfast nor unambiguous. For example, pests may be direct pests in one crop and indirect pests in another, or they can be both direct and indirect pests in different stages of their life cycle. In general, indirect pests affect yield and crop quality less severely than is the case for direct pests at any given level of pest density. For this reason they are more amenable to suppression through biological control. Most important for biological control are effects on produce quality. Unlike most indirect pests, direct pests by their nature affect both crop yield and quality. Thus, the farmer's harvest is ultimately reduced, and subsequent revenues are cut even further because of poor crop quality. The higher the premium paid for cosmetic qualities in a commodity, the harder it is for biological control to economically outcompete other control methods. Therefore targeting "indirect" pests is preferred in our index. Vectors of important plant diseases that affect either plant survival or the harvested portion of the plant should be viewed as direct pests in our system, as opposed to vectors of less virulent plant diseases or vectors of diseases that affect only the nonharvested portion of the plant; e.g., the foliage of some fruit and vegetable crops.

Although the terms direct and indirect are widely accepted for pests in many commodity groups, some authors have suggested other approaches for commodities such as ornamental plants. Raupp et al. (1988), for example, have suggested the measurement of aesthetic damage as the main component in assessing the effect of pests on ornamental plants. Accordingly in our index, pests of ornamental crops are evaluated based on their aesthetic effect. For the purposes of evaluation, we consider pests causing low aesthetic damage as better biological control targets than those that cause high aesthetic damage.

Cost of Using Biological Control. Finally, the cost and duration of a possible biological control project is considered in our economic assessment index. Project duration and complexity were considered of prime importance. Less complex, shorter projects are preferred to longer, more resource-consuming ones. In projects involving options other than classical biological control, the availability of commercially produced agents may make their use in a biological control program relatively inexpensive and fast. Use of these agents is also given priority because it may provide simpler, shorter, and relatively inexpensive biological control. This, of course, assumes that the correct species of natural enemy is commercially available, of good quality, and at a price competitive with other forms of control. Similarly, we give priority in our index to projects involving the redistribution of biological control agents that have been proven effective elsewhere. When agents are known but have not been introduced, project cost and duration are increased because of the need to complete important initial phases of the project such as foreign exploration, importation, and colonization. Projects requiring large rearing programs and repeated releases of natural enemies are costly and complex. These projects require long and steady commitments; therefore, we assume that they would be undertaken only under special circumstances where economic success is very likely under the limitations of existing knowledge. It should be noted that, for newly introduced pests, most of the economic loss posed by the pest will be potential rather than actual because the pest will not yet have occupied all of the cropping area. Thus the economic importance of a new pest, although hard to document, must be estimated from its impact in initially infested areas and with adjustments for the size of the total area at risk.

Institutional/Administrative Capabilities Assessment

The institutional/administrative assessment requires information on facilities and personnel as well as the desirability and limitations of alternative control methods. Scores can range from 0 to 13. The issues incorporated in the index to evaluate institutional capacity and administrative and political constraints address three questions: (1) Can the

Table 2. Assessment scores for Maryland landscape pests

Question	EUS	ELB	OBS	SRM	EFL	TM
	Biological control feasibility (16 points)					
1	1	1	0	0	1	1
2	1	1	1	1	1	1
3	1	1	1	1	1	1
4	1	1	1	0	1	0
5	1	1	0	1	0	0
6	2	2	0	0	0	0
7	3	2	0	0	0	0
8	3	2	0	3	0	0
Total	12	11	3	6	4	3
	(16)	(14)	(4)	(8)	(5)	(4)
	Economic assessment (18 points)					
A-1	0	2	2	0	0	0
B-1	2	2	2	1	0	0
B-2	2	1	1	1	1	2
B-3	1	1	1	1	2	2
B-4	2	1	1	0	0	0
B-5	1	1	1	1	2	2
B-6	0	1	0	1	1	1
C-1	2	3	0	1	0	0
Total	10	12	8	6	6	7
	(11)	(13)	(10)	(7)	(4)	(8)
	Institutional/administrative assessment					
A-1	1	1	1	0	0	0
A-2	1	1	0	0	0	0
A-3	0	0	0	0	0	0
A-4	1	1	1	1	1	0
A-5	1	0	0	0	0	0
A-6	1	1	0	1	0	0
B-1	0	1	0	0	0	0
B-2	0	0	0	0	0	0
B-3	0	0	0	0	0	0
B-4	1	1	1	1	1	1
B-5	0	0	1	0	0	0
Total	6	6	4	3	2	1
	(10)	(10)	(6)	(5)	(3)	(2)

EUS, euonymus scale, *Unaspis euonymi* Comstock; ELB, elm leaf beetle, *Xanthogaleruca luteola* (Muller); OBS, obscure scale, *Melanaspis obscura* (Comstock); SRM, southern red mite, *Oligonychus ilicis* (McGregor); EFL, European fruit lecanium, *Parthenolecanium corni* (Bouche); TM, Taxus mealybug, *Dysmicoccus wisteriae* (Green). Values in parentheses represent the maximum scores in the weighted scale. The weighted scores can be compared across the three components of the index. The higher the score, the higher the priority the pest would have in the selection of a candidate for biological control. Totals are the total raw scores for each pest and the total weighted scores, in parentheses.

biological control project be accomplished and what resources will be needed to do so? (2) What alternative control strategies are available? (3) What are the external pressures urging action?

Conclusions. The index proposed in this paper, the criteria used therein, and the conclusions we have drawn about the use of the index are not presented as the ultimate solution to the problem of setting priorities. We do, however, present the index as an initial attempt to develop a working technique that will, hopefully, be modified and improved as it is used. We believe that our selection index will allow the biological control practitioner or program coordinator to identify areas of strength and weakness, as well as critical information gaps, in proposed biological control projects. For example, if the potential target pest is identified as one whose population dynamics are poorly understood, these studies might be earmarked as a high priority to be conducted before or concurrently with the project. Similarly, the index forces evaluation of one's capacity to undertake a biological control project. For example, completing the institutional/administrative assessment will determine if the required lines of cooperation and agreement among various agencies exist and if facilities, staffing levels, and funding are adequate. The use of the index may also bring to light certain critical incompatibilities, such as when the institutional/administrative assessment assigns high priority to a candidate target pest but the biological feasibility score for the species is low. Finally, as an example of the application of our index in Table 2 we provide index scores for six ornamental pests which are shown to be either highly suitable, moderately suitable, or relatively unsuitable candidates for biological control.

Acknowledgements

We thank Roy Van Driesche for the opportunity to write this paper. We are grateful for the comments, during the early phases of this project, of F. D. Bennett (Department of Entomology and Nematology, University of Florida, Gainesville), L. E. Ehler (Department of Entomology, University of California, Davis), R. W. Fuester (USDA ARS, Beneficial Insects Research Laboratory, Newark, Delaware), J. R. Fuxa (Department of Entomology, Louisiana State University, Baton Rouge), J. V. Maddox (Illinois Natural History Survey, Champaign), R. J. O'Neil (Department of Entomology, Purdue University, West Lafayette, IN), R. S. Soper (USDA ARS, National Program Staff), R. G. Van Driesche (Department of Entomology, University of Massachusetts, Amherst), and J. Waage (International Institute for Biological Control, CAB,

Silwood Park, UK). We also thank Norm Leppla and E.S. Delfosse (both USDA APHIS National Biological Control Institute) for their encouragement and support. The work reported here was financially supported by the National Biological Control Institute. Scientific article A6297, Contribution No.8468, of the Maryland Agricultural Experiment Station, Department of Entomology.

References Cited

Bennett, F. D. 1974. Criteria for the determination of candidate hosts and for selection of biotic agents, pp. 87-96. *In* F. G. Maxwell & F. A. Harris [eds.], Proceedings of the summer institute on biological control of plants, insects and diseases. University Press of Mississippi, Jackson.

Carl, K. P. 1982. Biological control of native pests by introduced natural enemies. Biocontrol News and Information. 3: 191-200.

Cock, M. J. W. 1986. Requirements for biological control: an ecological perspective. Biocontrol News and Information. 7: 7-16.

Ehler, L. E. & J. C. Miller. 1978. Biological control in temporary agroecosystems. Entomophaga 23: 207-212.

Ehler, L. E. & L. A. Andres. 1983. Biological control: exotic natural enemies to control exotic pests, pp. 395-418. *In* C. L. Wilson & C. L. Graham [eds.], Exotic Plant Pests and North American Agriculture. Academic, New York.

Ervin, R. T., L. J. Moffitt & D. E. Meyerdirk. 1983. Comstock mealybug (Homoptera: Pseudococcidae): cost analysis of a biological control program in California. J. Econ. Entomol. 76: 605-609.

Force, D. C. 1974. Ecology of insect host-parasitoid communities. Science 184: 624-632.

Gill, S. 1989. Central Maryland horticulture survey report. Cooperative Extension Service. University of Maryland, College Park.

Greathead, D. J. 1986. Parasitoids in classical biological control, pp. 289-318. *In* J. K. Waage & D.J. Greathead [eds.], Insect parasitoids. Academic, New York.

Greathead D. J. & J. K. Waage. 1983. Opportunities for biological control of agricultural pests in developing countries. World Bank Technical Paper 11.

Hall, R. W. & L. E. Ehler. 1979. Rate of establishment of natural enemies in classical biological control. Bull. Entomol. Soc. Am. 26: 280-282.

Harris, P. 1979. Cost of biological control of weeds in Canada. Weed Sci. 27: 242-250.

Harris, P. 1984. Current approaches to biological control of weeds, pp. 95-103. *In* J. S. Kelleher & M.A. Hulme [eds.], Biological control programmes against insects and weeds in Canada. Commonwealth Agriculture Bureaux. Slough, U.K.

Headley, J. C. 1985. Cost benefit analysis: defining research needs, pp. 53-63. *In* M. A. Hoy & D.C. Herzog [eds.]. Biological control in agricultural IPM systems. Academic, New York.

Hokkanen, H. M. T. 1985. Success in biological control. CRC Crit. Rev. Plant Sci.3: 35-72.

Hoy, M. A. 1985. Improving establishment of arthropod natural enemies, pp. 151-166. *In* M. A. Hoy & D.C. Herzog [eds.]. Biological control in IPM systems. Academic, New York.

Huffaker, C. B., F. J. Simmons & J. E. Laing. 1976. The theoretical and empirical basis of biological control, pp. 41-78. *In* C. B. Huffaker & P.S. Messenger [eds.]. Theory and practice of biological control. Academic, New York.

Lloyd, D. C. 1960. The significance of the type of host plant crop in successful biological control of insect pests. Nature (Lond.) 187: 430-431.

Maryland Department of Agriculture. 1989. Maryland agricultural statistics: summary for 1988. Maryland Agricultural Statistics Service, Maryland Department of Agriculture, Annapolis.

Maryland Department of Agriculture. 1990. Maryland agricultural statistics: summary for 1989. Maryland Agricultural Statistics Service, Maryland Department of Agriculture, Annapolis.

McClay, A. S. 1989. Selection of suitable target weeds for classical biological control in Alberta. Alberta Environmental Centre, Vegreville, AECV89-R1.

Raupp, M. J., J. A. Davidson, C. S. Koehler, C. S. Sadof & K. Reichelderfer. 1988. Decision-making considerations for aesthetic damage caused by pests. Bull. Entomol. Soc. Am. 34: 27-32.

Reichelderfer, K. H. 1981. Economic feasibility of biological control of crop pests, pp. 403-417. *In* G. C. Papavisas [ed.], Biological control in crop production. Allenhead/Osmun, Totowa, NJ.

Southwood, T.R.E. 1977. The relevance of population dynamic theory to pest status, pp. 35-54. *In* J. M. Cherrett & G. R. Sagar [eds.], Origins of pest, parasite, disease and weed problems. Blackwell, Oxford.

Tisdell, C. A. 1990. Economic impact of biological control of weeds and insects, pp. 301-316. *In* M. Mackauer, L.E. Elher & J. Roland [eds.], Critical issues in biological control. Intercept, Andover, U.K.

Turnbull, A. L. & D. A. Chant. 1961. The practice and theory of biological control of insects in Canada. Can. J. Zool. 39: 697-753.

USDA–ARS. 1984. Research planning conference on biological control, March 20-22, 1984, Laurel, MD. U.S. Government Printing Office, Washington, DC.

   1988. ARS national biological control program. Proceedings of a workshop on research priorities, July 14-15, 1987, Beltsville, MD. U.S. Government Printing Office, Washington, DC.

U.S. Department of Commerce. 1987. Census of agriculture: Maryland, state and county data, vol.1, part 20. AC87-A-20. U.S. Department of Commerce, Washington, DC.

Van Driesche, R. G. & E. Carey. 1987. Opportunities for increased use of biological control in Massachusetts. Mass. Exp. Stn. Res. Bull. 718. Amherst.

Van Emden, H. F. 1989. Plant diversity and natural enemy efficiency in agroecosystems, pp. 63-80. *In* M. Mackauer, L.E. Ehler & J. Roland [eds.], Critical issues in biological control. Intercept, Andover, U.K.

Van Emden, H. F. & G. F. Williams. 1974. Insect stability and diversity in agroecosystems. Annu. Rev. Entomol. 19: 455-475.

Waage, J. K. 1989. Ecological theory and the selection of biological control agents, pp. 135-157. *In* M. Mackauer, L.E. Ehler & J. Roland [eds.], Critical issues in biological control. Intercept, Andover, U.K.

Waterhouse, D. F. & K. R. Norris. 1987. Biological control: Pacific prospect. Australian Centre for International Agricultural Research. Inkata, Melborne.

Watt, K.E.F. 1965. Community stability and the strategy of biological control. Can. Entomol. 94: 887-895.

Foreign Exploration

T. S. Bellows, Jr., and E. F. Legner

Department of Entomology, University of California, Riverside, CA 92521

ABSTRACT

Foreign exploration programs may be divided into three phases: (1) selecting favorable search locations, (2) planning the exploration, and (3) conducting the exploration. The first phase involves the use of biogeographical information on the target species and its relatives to identify locations likely to provide efficient natural enemies. The second phase involves planning the travel itinerary, contacting colleagues in areas to be searched to obtain advice and arrange for assistance, and coordination with a quarantine facility to process collected material when it is shipped to the home country. The final phase involves conducting the travel, searching for natural enemies, processing the field collected material, and shipping collected material to the quarantine facility.

The discovery of exotic natural enemies and their introduction to new locations to suppress pest populations has long been a significant part of biological control and, worldwide, has repeatedly proved valuable in reducing or eliminating pest problems (DeBach 1964a, Laing & Hamai 1976, Clausen 1978, Julien 1987). The objective of this tactic is to introduce effective species or strains of natural enemies into desired areas to attack and suppress pest populations. The approach has been applied in a wide variety of natural, agricultural, and urban settings. Introduced natural enemies have included vertebrates, invertebrates, and microbes that have been deployed against pest plants, arthropods, mollusks, vertebrates, and plant diseases. The potential for control of many pest organisms in diverse environments using introduced natural enemies is substantial; consequently, there is a significant and continued need for the skilled practice of foreign exploration to locate and secure new natural enemies. Our paper reviews practical methods for increasing the effectiveness of the foreign exploration process.

Several steps are necessary for the successful development of an exploration program, the duration of which may span several years or decades. These may be grouped into three phases of a project: (1) selecting favorable search locations, (2) preparing for the exploration trip, and (3) conducting the exploration. Exploration programs are best viewed as a continuing process of natural enemy introductions over a span of time rather than as a single foreign exploration event. Many of the technical and biological considerations relative to acquiring and shipping biological agents are similar regardless of the taxonomic group of natural enemies being collected (Bartlett & van den Bosch 1964, Boldt & Drea 1980, Klingman & Coulson 1983, Schroeder & Goeden 1986, & Coulson & Soper 1989). In this paper we consider in turn the three phases of a foreign exploration program.

Selecting Favorable Search Locations

Two paradigms for searching for natural enemies of particular pests have been proposed, and both have met with success. The first of these is to search for natural enemies on the target pest, usually in what is presumed to be the native home of an introduced pest. The second is to search for natural enemies, not on the target pest, but on species which are either taxonomically related to the pest or that occupy similar ecological niches.

Searching in the Pest's Native Home. The first strategy is founded on the premise that natural enemy-host associations in locations where the host is native or endemic will be characterized by efficient natural enemies. Many dramatic successes in biological control, where the population density of the target pest is permanently reduced below economically damaging levels, have involved the introduction of one or more species of natural enemy from the presumed native home of the pest (Franz 1961a,b; DeBach 1964b, 1974; van den Bosch 1971; Hagen & Franz 1973; Clausen 1978; Franz & Krieg 1982; Luck 1982). One early and widely known success, the control of cottony cushion scale, *Icerya purchasi* Maskell, by *Cryptochetum iceryae* (Williston) and *Rodolia cardinalis* (Mulsant) followed this pattern (Quezada & DeBach 1973). Cottony cushion scale invaded California, and effective natural enemies were found in its native range (southern Australia). This success established the pattern of introducing natural enemies from the presumed native range of exotic pests. Wide application of this approach resulted in many successful cases (DeBach 1964b), including biological control of Klamath weed, *Hypericum perforatum* L., in the United States; *Opuntia* spp. cacti in India and Australia; olive scale, *Parlatoria oleae* (Colvée); walnut aphid, *Chromaphis juglandicola* (Kaltenbach); Comstock mealybug, *Pseudococcus comstocki* (Kuwana) (Erwin et al.

1983); the whitefly *Siphoninus phillyreae* (Haliday) and many more (DeBach 1964b). This approach has been used successfully in both stable and unstable habitats (Ehler & Miller 1978, Hall et al. 1980) and is typically considered one of the first and best approaches for the control of an exotic pest that has recently invaded an area.

The first step in identifying a productive search area under this paradigm is to identify geographic regions where the introduced pest species might be native and where potentially effective natural enemy species or complexes might exist. In a few cases, this might be accomplished by direct reference to the literature on the target species, particularly if it has been the object of prior biological control research. For biological control it may be sufficient to identify a place of recent origin of a species, or the place from which it was introduced into a particular country, to locate suitable natural enemies, even though this place may not represent the original native range of the species. In this context, the term "recent" might represent a few hundred or thousand years. The region of recent origin is known without doubt for some species because their invasions into certain areas have been noted historically. Examples of species in which the histories of some past invasions are known include cottony cushion scale; Klamath weed; *Opuntia* spp. cacti in India and Australia; European rabbit, *Oryctolagus cuniculus* (L.) in Australia; a eucalyptus snout beetle, *Gonipterus scutellatus* Gyllenhal; the fungi *Ceratocystis ulmi* (Boisman) C. Moreau (Dutch elm disease) and *Endothia parasitica* (Murriu) Anderson & Anderson (chestnut blight); olive scale; walnut aphid; navel orangeworm, *Amyelois transitella* (Walker); grape leaf skeletonizer, *Harrisina brillians* Barnes & McDunnough; and many more.

Frequently, however, little is known about the geographic origins of a particular introduced species. In such cases, combining historical and current information on the distribution of the pest and related species, its host plants, and its natural enemies can provide valuable clues for locating potentially productive search areas. Such biogeographical information can be used in five distinct ways to help identify potential search areas. These include the center of the current or historical geographic distribution of the species, the area where an abundance of related (congeneric) species exists, the area where the preferred or principal host plant originated, the number of natural enemies or number of host-specific natural enemies in an area, and the area where the pest is present but kept at low densities by natural enemies.

The center of distribution of a species can be a valuable clue to a productive search location, especially if the species has not become widely distributed. Hence, a species with limited historical distribution that suddenly appears, as introduced, in a widely disparate location will have a well-defined native region, specifically its historical distribution.

To identify the pest accurately and for help in identifying its native range, it is most useful to seek the help of taxonomists specializing in the taxon to which the target pest belongs. Important information about the geographical distribution of a species often may be obtained from species catalogs, publications on regional flora or fauna, and collection records of previous explorers. Such unpublished information may be available in institutional records, including those of various quarantine facilities (Dysart 1981, Coulson 1992). Inquiries of major world or regional museums or experiment station entomologists may provide useful information; Bull (1986) lists many public arthropod collections from around the world. The importance of proper taxonomic identifications (of both the target organism and of records in the literature) is crucial in this phase of the program, and all notations of the occurrence of a species should be viewed with caution because identifications, particularly historical ones, may differ substantially among locations or from the names of modern targeted species. Often a combination of information will lead to the conclusion about the native range of a species.

Such an approach can be used even for species currently with cosmopolitan distributions if adequate historical records exist. Citrus whitefly, *Dialeurodes citri* Ashmead, for example, has a current distribution which includes North America, the Caribbean region, parts of Central and South America, the Mediterranean Region, and the Near, Middle, and Far East. However, when Woglum (1913) conducted exploration for natural enemies earlier in this century, he did not find the species in the Mediterranean, near East, or in Malaysia (where it is still absent), but he did find it in India. Early collection records indicate the species was present also in the Far East early in this century. Hence, the likely conclusion about its native range is the subtropical Far East.

Although much can be inferred about the recent history of species from studies of their present range and recent changes in distribution, the fossil record may provide an important source for inferring origins over longer time periods. For example, the staphylinid beetle *Oxytelus gibbulus* Eppelsheim is currently restricted to the western Caucasus Mountains, even though fossil records show that it was abundant in Britain during the last glaciation. The western Caucasus, then, probably represents the location of a relict population of a once widespread species rather than its place of origin.

The number of species in a genus in particular areas can be used as a clue to the center of distribution of a particular group; this may prove valuable in identifying the potential native home for members of the genus or species group. For example, the greatest number of species of *Dialeurodes* occurs in the Far East, further supporting this area as a likely native region for citrus whitefly. Exceptions may arise, however. The concentration of species in a particular area may reflect their common environmental needs more than their center of origin or possibly radiation following colonization.

The distribution of a preferred host plant may also provide information on suitable locations for exploration for natural enemies as was the case in the search for natural enemies of California red scale, *Aonidiella aurantii* Maskell. Although explorations for natural enemies of this scale were conducted in the Far East, the Neotropics, and Africa, the most effective natural enemies were found in southern China and Pakistan, which are areas close to the likely native range of *Citrus*, the preferred host of the scale (Kennett et al. 1994).

A large complex of natural enemies also is believed to indicate the site of longest residence (native home) of a species, especially if one or more natural enemies are host specific. Information on natural enemy fauna are not commonly associated with literature records for species which are not pests and hence are less widely available at the outset of most foreign exploration programs. However, such information can be accumulated as explorations are conducted in different areas and can prove valuable in defining promising areas for further searching.

Areas where a species is kept under sufficient biological control so that it does not normally come to the notice of entomologists will be reported in the literature less frequently than areas where a species reaches damaging levels. Records of areas where a species is present but is not at pest levels may be accumulated during travels and may help identify such locations. Comparison of museum records and literature reports of pest status may also provide clues to the presence of a natural enemy fauna. When museum records indicate a species is present in a location where it is not reported as a pest, this may indicate the presence of effective natural enemies.

These five approaches for identifying favorable search areas are frequently used together. The amount of information supporting any particular approach may be limited, but all available information taken together may provide a fairly clear picture of promising areas for search. Once such regions have been identified, specific search locations within these regions can be selected by considering additional criteria, including accessibility and climatic or ecological similarity to the target area. However, such criteria are not absolute prerequisites for successful foreign exploration for effective natural enemies.

Searching for Natural Enemies of Related Species. In a number of cases, successful biological control has been accomplished by natural enemies originating from areas outside the native home of the attacked species, either from taxonomically related hosts or species that occupy similar ecological niches. This is well illustrated by the destruction of the American elm, *Ulmus americana* L. (native to North America) by the accidentally introduced fungus *Ceratocystis ulmi* (native to the Eastern

Hemisphere and vectored primarily by the European beetle *Scolytus multistriatus* (Marsham)) and the near-elimination of the American chestnut, *Castanea dentata* (Marsham) Borkhauser (native to North America), by the fungus *Endothia parasitica* (of Asian origin). Equally dramatic population reductions have occurred from intentional introduction programs such as the suppression of European rabbit populations by an intentionally introduced myxomatosis virus of South American origin; control of the black scale, *Saisettia oleae* (Olivier) (of probable northern African origin) by *Metaphycus helvolus* (Compere) (from extreme southern Africa; and suppression of *Oxydia trychiata* (Guenée) in Colombia by *Telenomus alsophilae* Viereck from eastern North America (Bustillo & Drooz 1977, Drooz et al. 1977). In some cases, the natural enemy has been collected from a taxonomically unrelated species which occupied a similar ecological niche. For example, the sugarcane borer, *Diatraea saccharalis* (F.) (Lepidoptera), of the Neotropical Region was suppressed by *Cotesia flavipes* (Cameron) from northern India, a parasitoid of stem-boring Coleoptera (Alam et al. 1971).

Thus, it may prove fruitful to adopt a wide search program to secure effective natural enemies, particularly when searching in presumed native regions is not productive. The problems in undertaking such a wider program, however, are somewhat greater than in a program with a more limited search area and species target. The search must now be made with a broad ecological image of the target. The resulting range of locations and possible hosts to examine becomes much larger and may involve considerable effort in both searching and in screening natural enemies for their effectiveness in controlling the target pest.

Although there are examples of control or suppression of a host by natural enemies without prior or recent association with the host, there are also numerous examples in which natural enemies from taxonomically related hosts, when exposed to the target host, failed to accept it as host or prey (Turnbull & Chant 1961). Furthermore, there are many examples of host reduction in which natural enemies were obtained from the native home of the pest species. Thus, contrary to suggestions by Hokkanen & Pimentel (1984), emphasis on the native home as a location to search for effective natural enemies should not be reduced. An analysis by Waage (1990) concludes that natural enemies drawn from the native range of a pest are more likely to provide control than agents with no previous contact with the host. Goeden & Kok (1986) and Schroeder & Goeden (1986) make similar assertions with respect to agents for the biological control of weeds.

Summary Concerning Search Locations. Productive searches can take place both within and outside the presumed native range of the target pest. Furthermore, it may be important to search with both a taxonomic and an ecological view of the target organism so that searches may include natural enemies of closely related organisms or taxonomically unrelated organisms that occupy similar ecological niches. Searches should include different seasons, elevations, and climates because the natural enemy fauna in each may vary significantly. Importations of populations of the same natural enemy species should be made from different areas to include possible cryptic races or biotypes. Searches for natural enemies should include candidates attacking any life stage of the target species. Finally, exploration is a continuing process which may require considerable long-term effort to secure suitable natural enemies.

Planning and Preparation

Permits, Regulations, Quarantine Facilities. The first steps in planning and organizing an exploration trip are to obtain the permits necessary to import the collected material and to coordinate with an authorized importation quarantine facility for processing the shipped material. Importation permits may be required by both national and local (state or provincial) agencies. Separate permits may be required for importation into quarantine and for release from quarantine (as is the case in the United States). Planning with the quarantine facility must cover expected dates of shipments; arrangements for customs clearance of shipped material; and agreements on expectations for handling, sorting, and subsequent shipping of natural enemies to the researcher. Export permits may be required to ship organisms out of some countries (e.g., Australia, Brazil, China). These should be arranged before the collecting trip is undertaken through local cooperating scientists or government officials. Requests for assistance can usually be directed to the national Ministry of Agriculture or its equivalent in each country.

Funding. Programs of foreign exploration require long-term, stable funding. A minimum of 12–18 mo. of preparation is often required to organize a collection trip, and the explorer must have assurance that funds will be available when the trip finally is conducted. In addition to funds required during the actual travel and exploration, funds should be budgeted for technical staff in the home institution to handle shipped material while the explorer is overseas, for development and maintenance of host colonies for a period of several months before and after the exploration, and for subsequent maintenance of any imported natural enemies. Budgets may also need to allow for contract services or support at the cooperating quarantine institution.

Adequate funds should be budgeted to cover the explorer's anticipated travel and subsistence costs, unanticipated travel, fees and subsistence for local guides, air transport for shipped material, and local purchases of supplies. In some countries, local travel to and from field sites must be provided by official government drivers, and funds for this service must also be incorporated into the planning process. Funds should be available to reimburse colleagues for personal expenses (i.e., gasoline or automobile costs, accommodation, etc.) incurred while accompanying the explorer. Additional funding is often desirable to establish cooperative projects with colleagues in foreign locations to ensure a larger collection, collection over a more extended season, or collection over more habitats than may be possible during the time the explorer is present.

Sources of funding might include national and state or provincial governments, commodity groups, experiment stations, or universities. A full-time person might be hired to carry out biology field studies abroad, as is currently practiced by USDA–ARS in biological weed control.

The Explorer/Collector. The explorer must have a broad knowledge of the targeted pest, its natural enemies, and related species. This information should include geographic and host ranges, host plants, biology, and taxonomy. Foreign exploration has often been conducted by permanent, full-time staff hired for this purpose. In addition, these duties have been undertaken by academic or professional-grade staff from state or federal agriculture experiment stations or other agencies; these staffs usually comprise scientists already working on the target pest or its close relatives.

The explorer must be prepared to travel under difficult circumstances. A knowledge of the languages and customs of the areas where explorations are to be conducted is important; if they are not readily available, services of local persons to assist with travel, communication, and coordination with government officials should be arranged.

Because of institutional constraints that require research, publication and teaching, university academic appointees often may not be able to spend the time required to search for and study targeted pests or natural enemies thoroughly in the field in foreign countries. Similar constraints may limit the ability of foreign colleagues to search for and ship the desired natural enemies. However, the cooperation of colleagues or contacts in the area selected for search is highly important in maximizing the efficient use of the often limited time available to an explorer in an area. A cooperative, continuing project, perhaps including the employment of a student for collecting and shipping natural enemies, may offer an excellent solution to obtaining material on a season-long basis. Some organizations, such as the International Institute of Biological Control (IIBC), United States Agricultural Research Service (USDA–ARS) and the Australian Commonwealth Scientific Industrial Research Organization (CSIRO), maintain laboratories in various countries for the purpose of collecting biological control agents. Collectors may be able to make arrangements with such laboratories for assistance in their work (Sailer 1974). The USDA–ARS, for example, maintains laboratories in France, Argentina, Korea, and China for such activities.

Collections of natural enemies for a particular program may also be obtained through the services of intermediary organizations. USDA–ARS will respond to requests for natural enemy collection and shipment from U.S. collaborators. Other international organizations such as IIBC also provide such services. However, personal experiences (T.S.B. and colleagues' unpublished data) suggest that biological control workers who know what they need and who physically participate in the collecting process may be more successful in obtaining natural enemies suitable for introduction.

Planning the Trip. Before departure on a collecting trip, a detailed itinerary should be developed for use in coordination with the quarantine facility and other staff involved in the program. Passports and visas must be obtained, often significantly in advance; for some countries this may require letters of cooperation or requests from national or provincial officials.

Contact with foreign collaborators can provide valuable information on suitable seasons and locations to be included in the exploration and can help arrange the hiring of guides in areas where they are needed.

The use of an itinerary in planning does not preclude alterations in the itinerary once the trip is underway. However, the itinerary should include days and times to expect shipments and, if possible, dates and times for planned contact by telephone, FAX, or telegram. These should be planned on a frequent basis to apprise the staffs of the quarantine facility and home institution on developments and changes in the expected dates of shipments and other itinerary changes.

Conducting the Exploration. The initial stages of setting up a foreign exploration trip typically involve a literature search, taxonomic study of museum material and voucher specimens from previous importations, review of explorers' notes from earlier trips dealing with the same or related pests, and correspondence with collaborators abroad concerning the best season to search. The latter include referrals from colleagues, local agricultural extension people, botanists, botanic gardens, nature preserves (especially in the search area), and a letter of introduction from the host country's consulate to institutions requesting their cooperation and, ideally, temporary use of their facilities.

As discussed above, permits must be obtained from appropriate agencies (in the United States, this includes state and federal (USDA–APHIS) agencies). Permits are required for importation into the home country and, in some cases, by the host country where regulations may govern the export of living as well as dead (museum) materials. Individual states or provinces may impose further restrictions or conditions.

Advance arrangements must be made with the receiving quarantine laboratory to assure timely availability of host material. The explorer should have a valid passport; necessary visas; immunization inoculations and records; letters of authorization from the host institution, USDA, and proper officials in the country of search showing names of cooperating institutions or individual collaborators or both; and a supply of personal business cards.

Travel. The fundamentals of travel for foreign exploration are not different in principal from those of any foreign travel. Nonetheless, some points require discussion.

Foreign explorers must travel "self-contained." Necessary supplies include drinking water, water purification tablets, medicine, and high-energy foods. Provision should be made especially for care of the feet (including antifungal medications because long hours of field work in hot climates will subject them to risk of infection) and for intestinal disorders which, although unlikely to be life-threatening, can lead to restrictions in travel and searching.

The expedition equipment must include a camera and all the necessary items for collections and shipment. Shipping materials may be difficult to find in the host country, so it is prudent to carry shipping containers, string, tape, labels, etc.

Based on a projected itinerary, the explorer should obtain all airplane, train, or boat tickets before leaving the home country because tickets can be extremely difficult to obtain in some locations. Nonetheless, the explorer must be flexible and prepared to alter the itinerary should circumstances (such as particularly productive or unproductive collecting in a particular location) warrant.

The collector must be able to pay promptly for expenses incurred. Fluctuating exchange rates can be a difficult problem to anticipate when making long range plans. Surges in the inflation rate can also create unexpected expenditures. Because of such contingencies, the collector is well advised to carry 20% more than estimated in the form of $20 or $50 travelers' checks. Internationally accepted credit cards also should be carried.

In some locations, it may be appropriate for the explorer to notify the embassy or consulate of his presence and local address to expedite communication from embassy officials should the need arise.

Foreign exploration often is conducted alone. Such travel can result in culture shock and a sense of isolation following an extended absence from familiar foods, languages, and surroundings. Such culture shock perhaps can be ameliorated by carrying familiar reading material, self-contained audio tape players and recordings, and familiar foods. For longer trips, a visit to an embassy or consulate can often provide familiar foods, newspapers, and other items that can offer a period of physical and mental refreshment. A day of rest each week can help prevent fatigue and its related loss of efficiency. Travel with a colleague can often prevent some of the more negative effects of such trips.

Collections. The assistance of a local entomologist can be invaluable in locating habitats or agricultural plantings suitable for collecting. Local graduate students often are excellent guides.

The explorer should collect as much material as possible. Searches are usually for native populations of natural enemies, and these may be at substantially lower densities than more familiar pest populations. Accurate field notes should be kept of the dates, exact locations, and stages of all insects collected, the names of local persons contacted, locations visited (including names of villages and farms), as well as descriptions of the types of habitats, plant communities, host plant species and host species examined, and the kinds and numbers of natural enemies found. Records should also be made of any other pests noticed in the collection areas that might serve as possible sources of natural enemies for other projects. Maps (obtained either in the home country or abroad) and photographs can be a valuable addition to the field journal and very helpful in precisely defining search locations. These records are especially valuable in planning future trips to the same area.

The explorer should be aware that constant field work may be more taxing than customary employment. Suitable precautions, such as carrying water in the field, wearing hats in warm climates, and not exceeding one's physical limits should be taken because they will be important in permitting continued, productive exploration.

Provisions should be made to maintain collected material in optimal condition while in the field. This usually will require a small, insulated ice chest or other similar container to limit variations in temperature, together with suitable collecting containers or media.

Processing Collected Material. Adequate time should be allowed daily for sorting and processing collected material for storage and shipment. Depending on the amount of material found in the field, time for processing collections may exceed the time spent collecting. Access to a local laboratory facility (e.g., an ARS or local university laboratory if available) can be invaluable in providing working space, lights, microscopes, etc., but in general the explorer should take all the materials and equipment necessary to process collections in a hotel room or similar accommodation.

Collected material should be shipped as frequently as necessary to ensure optimal condition of the material on arrival at the quarantine facility. Where possible, life stages that are least susceptible to the rigors of transport should be selected for shipment. Such stages would include pupae of holometabolous insects, larvae in diapause (and therefore not requiring food), or eggs, and for pathogens might include cadavers, spores, fungal hyphal colonies in agar, etc. Special provisions (such as ice packs, humidity-regulating materials, etc.) should be made in packaging the material where variations in temperature or humidity must be

Department of Entomology, University of California   S&R No._____
Exploration for entomophagous insects, etc.   Shipper's No. _____
Quarantine Facility, Riverside

SENDER'S REPORT

Country: _____   Shipper: _____
Shipping point: _____   Shipped to: _____
Date of shipment: _____   Remarks: _____
Transport: _____   _____
Packaging: _____   _____

Part	Host insect	Entomophagous species	Host plant	Collection locality	Date collected	Collector

Fig. 1. Example of a form used by foreign explorers of the University of California to record information on natural enemies collected outside of the United States and sent to the University of California Quarantine facility.

restricted during shipment. Additional details regarding packaging and shipping natural enemies are found in Bellows (1994) and Fisher & Andres (1994).

Shipping. Shipment of collected material should almost always take place by air freight or, if this is impossible, by airmail. Experience indicates that shipping via air freight is the preferred method, but the collector may have to hold material for several days pending return to a city with air freight service. Once in a city with such service, travel to an airport facility and making arrangements for shipping can require several hours, and substantial time should be planned for this in the itinerary. Arrangements at the airport can be complicated by language barriers, so the assistance of a local colleague (including ARS personnel where available) may be helpful. If airmail is the transport method, it is essential that the shipper witness application of stamps to the package and their hand cancellation (to prevent damage by mechanical cancellation machines) while at the foreign post office.

Material must be shipped before leaving one country and arriving at another unless the explorer has importation permits for the new country. When travel is by air, this will usually be straightforward because most airports provide shipment services for air cargo. When travel is by some other means, packages must be shipped via airmail. Some countries have exportation permits for shipments of natural enemies, which should be obtained (if possible) before leaving the home country.

If at all possible, air freight and airmail shipments should be dispatched at a time when the material will arrive in the home country from Monday through Thursday. This will facilitate rapid handling of the package and minimize delays, especially avoiding the delay characteristic of weekend arrivals. Personnel at the quarantine facility should be notified by telephone, telegram, or FAX regarding the shipment, including the expected carrier and routing, time of arrival, and the airway bill number, and should also be notified of changes in travel itinerary and expected shipment dates.

The external packaging material should bear the necessary permits and address labels to facilitate recognition and handling by customs and inspection personnel. Bellows (1994) provides details regarding labelling of contents, escape-proof wrapping, and affixing of proper shipping and importation labels. These procedures must be meticulously performed to avoid delay at the port-of-entry customs and agriculture inspection. Field notes and other documentation needed by quarantine personnel in processing shipments should be included in packages (Fig. 1) (see Coulson 1992, Bellows 1994, Ertle 1994 for details).

Assistance. The assistance of a local colleague (perhaps an associate, a former student of the collector, or ARS personnel where available) is essential for maximizing the productivity of the collection effort, especially if a relatively short stay in each location is available by prearranged travel itineraries, unexpected delays from local holidays or strikes, inclement weather, etc. Such a person can serve as guide, driver of a rental vehicle, and mentor regarding local customs. Local assistants can also expedite entry to private or public properties and assist in organizing the shipment of collections. Knowing the local language, your host will be able to allay suspicions or perhaps outright hostility of the local people toward the presence of a foreigner.

U.S. explorers who are federal employees on assigned overseas duty, such as USDA staff, may obtain official assistance at U.S. embassies. State and university employees are typically viewed by embassies as travelling citizens (because they are not federal employees) and typically cannot receive special privileges or assistance. However, inquiries at USDA or other international laboratories abroad can often yield useful information and assistance.

Conclusions. Foreign exploration is best viewed as a continuing process which requires a stable project for long-term development and success. Modern exploration will typically involve many trips in different seasons and areas. This type of intermittent travel provides opportunities for the discovery of natural enemies approximately equivalent to the long-term (months or years) continuous exploration of earlier workers which has played such a significant role in many successful projects. The establishment of cooperative relationships with colleagues overseas may allow longer-term collection and importation than is possible by a single researcher.

References Cited

Alam, M. M., F. D. Bennett & K. P. Carl. 1971. Biological control of *Diatraea saccharalis* (F.) in Barbados by *Apanteles flavipes* Cam. and *Lixophaga diatraeae* T.T. Entomophaga 16: 151–158.

Bartlett, B. R. & R. van den Bosch. 1964. Foreign exploration for beneficial organisms, pp. 283–304. *In* DeBach, P. [ed.], Biological control of insect pests and weeds. Chapman & Hall, London.

Bellows, T. S., Jr. 1994. Shipping natural enemies, pp. 43-51. *In* R. G. Van Driesche & T. S. Bellows, Jr., [eds], Thomas Say Publications in Entomology: Proceedings: Steps in Classical Arthropod Biological Control. Entomological Society of America, Lanham, MD.

Boldt, P. E. & J. J. Drea. 1980. Packing and shipping beneficial insects for biological control. FAO Plant Prot. Bull. 28: 64–71.

Bull, E. J. 1986. The insect and spider collections of the world. Flora & Fauna, Gainesville, FL.

Bustillo, A. E. & A. T. Drooz. 1977. Cooperative establishment of a Virginia (USA) strain of *Telenomus alsophilae* on *Oxydia trychiata* in Colombia. J. Econ. Entomol. 70: 767–770.

Clausen, C. P. [ed.]. 1978. Introduced parasites and predators of arthropod pests and weeds: a world review. USDA Agric. Handb. 480.

Coulson, J. R. 1992. Documentation of classical biological control introductions. Crop Prot. 11: 195–205.

Coulson, J. R. & R. S. Soper. 1989. Protocols for the introduction of biological agents in the United States, pp. 1–35. *In* R. P. Kahn [ed.], Plant protection and quarantine, vol. 3, special topics. CRC, Boca Raton, FL.

DeBach, P. 1964a. Biological control of insect pests and weeds. Reinhold, New York.

1964b. Successes, trends, and future possibilities, pp. 673–713. *In* P. DeBach [ed.], Biological control of insect pests and weeds. Reinhold, New York.

1974. Biological control by natural enemies. Cambridge University Press, London.

Drooz, A. T, A. E. Bustillo, G. F. Fedde & V. H. Fedde. 1977. North American egg parasite successfully controls a different host in South America. Science 197: 390–391.

Dysart, R. J. 1981. A new computer data bank for introduction and release of beneficial organisms, pp. 121–128, *In* G. C. Papavizas [ed.], Beltsville symposia in agricultural research. Vol. 5: Biological control in crop production, Granada, London.

Ehler, L. E. & J. C. Miller. 1978. Biological control in temporary agroecosystems. Entomophaga 23: 207–212.

Ertle, L. R. 1994. What quarantine does and what the collector needs to know, pp. 53-65. *In* R. G. Van Driesche & T. S. Bellows, Jr., [eds.], Thomas Say Publications in Entomology: Proceedings: Steps in Classical Arthropod Biological Control. Entomological Society of America, Lanham, MD.

Erwin, R. T., L. J. Moffitt & D. E. Meyerdirk. 1983. Comstock mealybug (Homoptera: Pseudococcidae): cost analysis of a biological control program in California. J. Econ. Entomol. 76: 605–609.

Fisher, T. W. & L. A. Andres. 1994. Quarantine: concepts, facilities, procedures. *In* T. W. Fisher et al. [eds.], Biological control: principles and applications. University of California Press, Berkeley.

Franz, J. M. 1961a. Biologische Schadlingsbekampfung, pp. 1–302. *In* P. Sorauer [ed.], Handbuch der Pflanzenkrankheiten, Band VI. Paul Parey, Berlin.

1961b. Biological control of pest insects in Europe. Annu. Rev. Entomol. 6: 183–200.

Franz, J. M. & A. Krieg. 1982. Biologische Schadlingsbekampfung 3 Auflage. Paul Parey, Berlin.

Goeden, R. D. & L. T. Kok. 1986. Comments on a proposed "new" approach for selecting agents for the biological control of weeds. Can. Entomol. 118: 51–58.

Hagen, K. S. & J. M. Franz. 1973. A history of biological control. Annu. Rev. Entomol. 18: 433–476.

Hall, R. W., L. E. Ehler & B. Bisabri-Ershadi. 1980. Rate of success in classical biological control of arthropods. Bull. Entomol. Soc. Am. 26: 111–114.

Hokkanen, H. & D. Pimentel. 1984. New approach for selecting biological control agents. Can. Entomol. 116: 1109–1121.

Julien, M. H. 1987. Biological control of weeds, a world catalogue of agents and their target weeds, 2nd ed. Commonwealth Agricultural Bureaux International, Wallingford, U.K.

Kennett, C. E., J. A. McMurtry & J. W. Beardsley. 1994. Biological control in subtropical and tropical crops. *In* T. W. Fisher et al. [ed.], Biological control: principles and applications. University of California Press, Berkeley.

Klingman, D. L. & J. R. Coulson. 1983. Guidelines for introducing foreign organisms into the United States for biological control of weeds. Weed Sci. 30: 661–667.

Klingman, D. L. & J. R. Coulson. 1983. Guidelines for introducing foreign organisms into the United States for biological control of weeds. Weed Sci. 30: 661–667.

Laing, J. E. & J. Hamai. 1976. Biological control of insect pests and weeds by imported parasites, predators and pathogens, pp. 685–743. *In* C. B. Huffaker & P. S. Messenger [eds.], Theory and practice of biological control. Academic, New York.

Luck, R. F. 1982. Parasitic insects introduced as biological control agents for arthropod pests, pp. 125–284. *In* D. Pimentel [ed.], CRC handbook of pest management in agriculture, Vol. 2. CRC, Boca Raton, FL.

Quezada, J. R. & P. DeBach. 1973. Bioecological and population studies of the cottony-cushion scale, *Icerya purchasi* Mask., and its natural enemies, *Rodolia cardinalis* Muls., and *Cryptochaetum iceryae* Will., in southern California. Hilgardia 41: 631–688.

Sailer, R. I. 1974. Foreign exploration and importation of exotic arthropod parasites and predators, pp. 97–109. *In* F. G. Maxwell & F. A. Harris [eds.], Proceedings of the Summer Institute on Biological Control of plants, insects and diseases. University of Mississippi Press, Jackson.

Schroeder, D. & R. D. Goeden. 1986. The search for arthropod natural enemies of introduced weeds for biological control—in theory and practice. Biocontr. News Info. 7(3): 147–155.

Turnbull, A. L. & D. A. Chant. 1961. The practice and theory of biological control of insects in Canada. Can. J. Zool. 39: 694-744.

van den Bosch, R. 1971. Biological control of insects. Annu. Rev. Ecol. Syst. 2: 45–66.

Waage, J. 1990. Ecological theory and the selection of biological control agents, pp. 135–157. *In* M. Mackauer L. E. Ehler & J. Roland [eds.], Critical issues in biological control. Intercept, Andover, U.K.

Woglum, R. S. 1913. Report of a trip to India and the orient in search of the natural enemies of the citrus white fly. USDA Bur. Entomol. Bull. 120.

Shipping Natural Enemies

T. S. Bellows, Jr.

Department of Entomology, University of California, Riverside, CA 92521

ABSTRACT

Shipping natural enemies is a critical part of many biological control activities (Bartlett & van den Bosch 1964, Boldt & Drea 1980, Fisher & Andres 1994). The successful shipping of natural enemies requires attention to three steps: (1) awareness of regulations governing the collection, export, and receipt of natural enemies in the countries of origin and destination; (2) selection of stages, packaging, and shipment of the natural enemies; (3) receipt of the shipment and clearance through customs and inspection personnel at the port of entry before shipment of the material to the quarantine facility responsible for handling the natural enemies. Advance planning and attention to these phases are valuable aids to the successful shipment of live natural enemies.

Regulations and Permits

Laws and regulations pertaining to the shipment and receipt of natural enemies vary among different countries. Some countries have no laws regulating the export of natural enemies, but others require such permits. Some countries have additional federal or provincial laws governing the collection of organisms. A valuable source for determining whether such permits are required is usually a colleague in the source country. Inquiries of the provincial or federal equivalents of ministries or departments of agriculture can also provide the necessary information about required permits.

Many countries regulate the receipt of shipments of insects or other natural enemies. In the United States there are no federal laws that specifically regulate the importation, movement, or release of natural enemies (Coulson & Soper 1989). Such activity is regulated by the interpretation of six federal statutes: (1) the Plant Quarantine Act, 1912 (the initial legislation to restrict movement of potential pests into the United States); (2) the Federal Plant Pest Act, 1957 (which regulates the importation and movement of plant pests and plant parts that may harbor pests); (3) the Public Health Services Act (which regulates the movement of insects and vectors of human disease agents); (4) the Federal Insecticide, Fungicide and Rodenticide Act (FIFRA) (which authorizes the Environmental Protection Agency to regulate pesticides and [by broad definition] biological control agents); (5) the National Environmental Policy Act (NEPA) (which requires an assessment of actions that may affect the quality of the environment); and (6) the Endangered Species Act (which attempts to avoid effects on indigenous rare and endangered species). The interpretation of these laws rests with the federal agency to which they are addressed. The regulation of importation at ports of entry and subsequent movement of shipments containing natural enemies into the United States rests with the Biological Assessment and Taxonomic Support Staff (APHIS–BATS), Plant Protection and Quarantine (PPQ), USDA–APHIS, Hyattsville, MD (Lima 1983). Many states also have regulations governing the movement and release of introduced organisms. Natural enemies are often regulated by interpretation of these regulations. The state authority for importation and other biological control activity usually resides in its Department of Agriculture.

The necessary permits for exporting live material from the country of origin and for importation into the target country should be obtained before shipping and, if appropriate, before exploration begins. Permits are required for all importations of live beneficial arthropods and microorganisms into the United States. Application for these permits is made on PPQ form 526 (Application and Permit to Move Live Plant Pests and Noxious Weeds). The completed forms are routed to PPQ through the state's authorizing agency in whose jurisdiction the receiving quarantine facility is located. Shipment labels are returned to the requesting agency and should be affixed to the outside of any shipments.

In the United States, PPQ recognizes three categories of organisms and regulates their importation accordingly:

Category A. Foreign plant pests not present or of limited distribution in the United States; domestic plant pests of limited distribution, including program pests; state-regulated pests; and exotic strains of domestic pests.

Category B. Biological control agents and pollinators. *B1.* High risk: weed antagonists; shipments accompanied by prohibited plant material or Category A pests. *B2.* Low risk: pure cultures of known beneficial organisms.

Category C. Domestic pests that have attained their ecological ranges, nonpest organisms and other organisms for which courtesy permits may be issued.

All exotic beneficial organisms (category B) entering the United States accompanied by category A pests (as hosts of the biological control agents) and all weed antagonists must be received in a primary PPQ-certified quarantine facility (Lima 1983).

In the case of weed-feeding arthropods and pathogens of weeds, the import application and labelling process is more complex than that for other natural enemies and includes two additional steps (Klingman & Coulson 1982). First, before filing a PPQ form 526, the applicant must prepare a proposal justifying the planned importation of the arthropod or pathogen for either study or release. The proposal must describe the importance of the weed problem and whether the target weed has any redeeming features that may lead to objections to its control, in addition to describing the organisms to be introduced (for either study or release). Information about the host range and biology of the organism must be summarized, and methods for its handling in quarantine must be described. The proposal is evaluated by the APHIS Technical Advisory Group (APHIS–TAG) which, after weighing the potential hazards and benefits, will authorize the importation or release, recommend further study, or decline to authorize the proposal. If the proposal is authorized, a completed PPQ form 526 and the proposal are submitted to the agricultural officials in whose state the primary quarantine facility or release site is located. When approved by the state, PPQ issues the importation labels. When the initial request is for study only, an additional proposal may be required by APHIS–TAG for authorization for release. The second step, required by APHIS–BATS before the initial release of an exotic weed biological control agent, is the preparation of an environmental assessment to meet the requirements of the National Environmental Policy Act (NEPA). These procedures are currently under evaluation for possible revision (Coulson et al. 1991, Charudattan & Browning 1992).

Packing and Shipping Natural Enemies

Shipments of natural enemies made before the advent of worldwide air travel often involved long distances over land and by sea. Shipments under such circumstances promoted the development of methods for prolonged sustenance of natural enemies, often including the maintenance of small insectary colonies on board ship and the selection for shipment of developmental stages least subject to mortality during shipment (Bartlett & van den Bosch 1964). Many of these methods are equally applicable to the more rapid shipment of natural enemies by air cargo or airmail.

Different stages of arthropod natural enemies vary in the physical and biotic conditions needed for their survival during shipping. Where possible, those stages with the fewest requirements for food or other sustenance should be chosen for shipping. Such stages include the adult, egg and pupal stages of the natural enemies themselves, and parasitized hosts in various life stages, provided these hosts will not themselves require food during shipping.

When eggs are shipped, they should be kept cool to minimize hatching as long as their survival is not jeopardized. Where eggs are attached to plant material, excess plant material should be removed. The plant substrate should be fastened securely in small containers or packed in layers separated by soft tissue to avoid movement that may cause the eggs to become dislodged from the substrate. Eggs, as with most other stages, should be packaged in several small containers (vials, petri dishes) rather than in one large container. Containers should be closed with nonabsorbent cotton, or if they are sealed, should contain some absorbent material to prevent condensation of moisture caused by changes in temperature during shipment.

Immature natural enemies in feeding stages (larvae or nymphs) and immature hosts bearing natural enemies pose special problems for shipping and should be avoided whenever possible. When such stages are found, it may be possible to remain in the area or to return at a time when such stages are nearing pupation. Alternatively, feeding stages of some groups may be collected by the explorer and fed until they pupate. These measures are undertaken because pupae are often shipped more success-fully (they do not require food and moisture resources in the shipment). When shipping immature or adult arthropods that are in actively feeding stages (such as larvae of Lepidoptera or adults or immatures of many predacious arthropods), individuals should be isolated in separate con-tainers to prevent cannibalism which can occur in many groups, particu-larly when food is scarce. Larvae or pupae in their insect hosts or in plant stems, roots, or other plant parts should be shipped *in situ* inside their host material. It may be necessary to provide actively feeding stages with a small amount of plant material on which to feed during transit. In these cases, individuals should be isolated in separate small vials or petri dishes and a small amount of food material should be provided. This may require special care in the shipping of plant parts to maintain the integrity of the plant material and prevent secondary bacterial and fungal growth on the plant tissue. After excess soil is removed, roots bearing natural enemies should be packed with lightly moistened sphagnum moss, wrapped in burlap and a cloth bag, and placed in an unwaxed cardboard or wooden container. To prevent excessive condensation of moisture, the material should not be enclosed in plastic. Plant leaf, stem, or flower galls containing actively feeding or developing stages can be packed with sphagnum moss or excelsior. Ample space should be provided to allow air circulation to prevent overheating and decomposition of materials. It may be advantageous to seal the ends of cut plant stems with melted paraffin. Some Heteroptera may be shipped as immatures or adults; predacious forms should be fed before shipping if possible.

Pupae should be divided into a number of small lots in separate containers rather than placed together in one large container. Lepidopteran pupae collected from the soil can be packed in slightly moistened sphagnum moss. Dipteran pupae extracted from soil can be repackaged in moist, sterilized soil in a series of small containers. Pupae on twigs or foliage or in cocoons on other substrates are best left attached to the substrate and packaged gently in shredded newsprint or sphagnum moss to prevent movement during shipping. Dried flower heads containing diapausing larvae or pupae can be shipped in bulk in cloth bags enclosed in a cardboard or wooden container. Natural enemies of sternorrhynchan homopterans are usually best shipped as pupae inside their hosts. Isolation of individual hosts is critical in these groups to prevent loss of pupae to parasitism by early-emerging females (many species of natural enemies of these groups produce male progeny as hyperparasites on female pupae). Bits of leaves or stems bearing these pupae can be placed in small vials, which can then be placed in groups in a styrofoam food container. Humidity can be somewhat controlled and desiccation of the material probably lessened, by enclosing (in the styrofoam container) a smaller container (petri dish) containing a saturated salt solution and sealed with a semipermeable membrane such as "OpSite" (Smith & Nephew Medical Limited, Hull, U.K.), a surgical burn dressing which is adhesive and seals such containers well and is available in pharmacies.

Adults of some natural enemies are sufficiently robust to be shipped, particularly when time in transit is minimal (<48 h). Adults should be provided with access to a moist, absorbent material during shipment, although care must be taken to prevent excessive moisture. Access to food is important for improved survival in some groups. Small spots of honey placed on the inside of the container often provide suitable food and are regularly fed upon by most adult Hymenoptera. Honey can also be added to vials containing pupae, so that any adults emerging during transit will have access to food. Access to sugar water or honey, either on the inside of the glass containers or on wicks of cotton or sponge, also should be provided for adult Lepidoptera and Diptera. Moistened raisins have also been used (Bartlett & van den Bosch 1964). Excess honey should be avoided when microhymenoptera are shipped because adults will become entrapped in honey droplets and killed. Pollen may be provided for adult predaceous mites. Adult Coleoptera can survive several days without food, particularly if they are well fed before shipment. A small amount of moistened and shredded wood, pipe cleaners, or other material can be provided as resting substrates for the adults. The use of wood shavings may be dangerous if they contain strong natural resins or have been treated with wood-preserving chemicals. This is especially true for predacious heteropterans.

Several guidelines (Fisher & Andres 1994) for the general packing and packaging of natural enemies for shipment can be provided, but common sense and experience will often provide details suitable for any particular situation. The least active stages of an organism (eggs, pupae, diapausing larvae, and adults) often survive the rigors of transport better than active stages. Extreme temperatures and undue amounts of time organisms must remain in the package are the principal causes of loss during shipment, and steps should be taken to minimize these. Fisher & Andres (1994) recommend cooling packages before shipment and taking steps to keep packages cool during shipment. Minimizing the amount of fresh plant material can be critical. Such material breaks down rapidly when packages are inadvertently exposed to sunlight or warmth, leading to death of natural enemies. It is also important to control the amount of free moisture in packages. Myers & Sabath (1981) recommend shipping organisms taken from expanding or healthy populations to minimize the risk of shipping diseased or genetically impoverished individuals. Early-season collections of multivoltine species may contain fewer parasites (including hyperparasites) than late-season generations.

Avoid using fresh plastic materials in shipping containers because they may be toxic to natural enemies. Avoid using gelatin capsules because they may extract moisture from the environment, contributing to desiccation of the material being shipped. In addition, gelatin capsules in humid environments may soften and collapse. Enclose groups of vials or other containers in closed styrofoam containers, cloth bags, or other additional wrapping. These secondary packages should be enclosed in an insulated container such as styrofoam and then in a robust shipping container of cardboard, wood, or other firm material. This final shipping container must contain shipping and permit labels, routing instructions, instructions for handling on arrival and telephone numbers for the primary quarantine facility. Some packages may benefit by including in the final package a frozen artificial ice pack or dry ice (where exceptional cold is warranted) to protect against excessive changes in temperature.

Often it is most practical for the explorer to take all necessary packaging and shipping materials on an exploration trip. In other circumstances, such materials must be acquired during the exploration trip.

Shipments should be made by the most direct secure routing, which usually means air freight or other express services such as international couriers. Delay sealing the package before shipment as long as possible. Contact (either by telephone, facsimile, or other method) should be made with the primary quarantine facility and the individual responsible for receipt of the shipment as soon as details of the routing, arrival time, and carrier are known. Shipments should be made only when they will arrive during a normal working day, because a shipment usually cannot be cleared through the port of entry except by personnel of the official interception agency. If necessary, shipment should be delayed in the country of origin until a suitable arrival time can be arranged. Each package should contain copies of all importation permits, documentation, and field notes needed by the staff of the quarantine facility receiving the material to identify the sender of the package and the origin and nature of the materials in the package.

Receiving Shipments from Abroad. The receipt and handling of shipments from abroad typically pose no serious problems if suitable arrangements are made sufficiently in advance. The principal concern is rapid clearance of the material through the official interception agency at the port of entry. Two general approaches are used: collection of the shipment directly by personnel from the receiving quarantine facility, or the use of a customs broker.

Where a point of entry is available near the receiving quarantine facility, every effort should be made to ship directly to this port of entry. Delays at points of entry far removed from the receiving quarantine, where experience in handling and clearing material may be limited, can be very costly. When material arrives at the port of entry, quarantine personnel can be contacted directly by the air cargo company and by personnel from the official intercepting agency (USDA–APHIS in the United States). In this way the material can be collected from the port of entry immediately upon arrival and taken directly to quarantine, thus minimizing delays. In addition, a long-term relationship between personnel at the interception agency and the receiving institution can develop, leading to efficient and rapid handling of shipments.

In cases where there is no port of entry that can be reached by direct shipment from abroad, shipments may be collected by a customs broker. The efficiency of this procedure depends largely on communicating to the broker the need for rapid handling. An experienced broker should have no difficulty in gaining permission to obtain the shipment and to immediately forward it (by courier or air cargo) to the receiving quarantine. Personnel at the receiving quarantine can facilitate this transfer by corresponding with the broker on official letterhead specifying his authority to collect the shipment, and by contacting personnel at the interception agency at the port of entry and explaining in advance the circumstances and particular details of the collection and subsequent shipment. In all cases, the continual development of working relationships with brokers and agency personnel will prove beneficial in improving efficiency for future shipments.

Shipping Within the United States. Some states govern the movement and release of arthropods in addition to the regulations imposed at the federal level. These include California, Florida, North Carolina, and Oregon. In these cases, APHIS-PPQ issues shipping labels at the request of the appropriate state agency through which permit requests (PPQ form 526) have been routed. Packages containing biological control agents shipped or mailed interstate should bear this label. State regulatory officials such as County Agricultural Commissioners and state Department of Agriculture personnel should be routinely informed of releases within their jurisdiction, whether or not permits are required.

Acknowledgments

Thanks go to Jan Nyrop (New York Agricultural Experiment Station, Geneva) who contributed a paper on this topic at the symposium at the Entomological Society of America Eastern Branch meetings in Baltimore in September 1990; and to Ted Fisher (Department of Entomology, University of California–Riverside) and Lloyd Andres (USDA –ARS, Albany, CA) for providing an unpublished copy of their manuscript.

References Cited

Bartlett, B. R. & R. van den Bosch. 1964. Foreign exploration for beneficial organisms, pp. 283–304. *In* P. DeBach [ed.], Biological control of insect pests and weeds, Chapman & Hall, London.

Boldt, P. E. & J. J. Drea. 1980. Packaging and shipping beneficial insects for biological control. FAO Plant Prot. Bull. 28(2): 64–71.

Charudattan, R. & H. W. Browning [eds.]. 1992. Regulations and guidelines: critical issues in biological control. Proceedings of a USDA/CSRS National Workshop, June 10–12, 1991, National Wildlife Federation Laurel Ridge Conservation Education Center, Vienna, VA. IFAS, Univ. Florida, Gainesville.

Coulson, J. R. & R. S. Soper. 1989. Protocols for the introduction of biological agents in the United States, pp. 1–35. *In* R. P. Kahn [ed.], Plant protection and quarantine, vol. 3., special topics. CRC, Boca Raton, FL.

Coulson, J. R., R. S. Soper & D. W. Williams [eds.]. 1991. Biological control quarantine: needs and procedures. Appendix III, Proposed ARS guidelines for introduction and release of exotic organisms for biological control, proceedings of a workshop. USDA–ARS-99.

Fisher, T. W. & L. A. Andres. 1994. Quarantine: concepts, facilities, procedures. *In* T. W. Fisher et al. [eds.], Biological control: principles and applications. University of California Press, Berkeley.

Klingman, D. L. & J. R. Coulson. 1982. Guidelines for introducing foreign organisms into the United States for biological control of weeds. Weed Sci. 30: 661–667.

Lima, P. J. 1983. Safeguard guidelines for containment of plant pests under permit. USDA–APHIS 81-61.(Rev. of 29 October 1979 memo).

Myers, J. H. & M. D. Sabath. 1981. Genetic and phenotypic variability, genetic variance, and the success of establishment of insect introductions for the biological control of weeds, pp. 91–102. *In* E. S. Delfosse [ed.], Proceedings of the Vth international symposium on biological control of weeds, Brisbane, Australia, 22–29 July 1980.

What Quarantine Does and What the Collector Needs To Know

Lawrence R. Ertle

Beneficial Insects Research Laboratory, USDA–ARS, Newark, DE 19713

ABSTRACT

Quarantine is a screening process intended to permit the introduction of desired exotic organisms into a new region while simultaneously excluding all undesirable contaminants. Contaminants to be excluded include arthropods, plant diseases, and other pests, parasitoids, and pathogens associated with or affecting the desired agents being introduced. Quarantine is achieved through use of buildings designed to prevent escape of undesired organisms and adherence by personnel to quarantine procedures. Foreign collectors enhance the effectiveness of quarantine through planning and consultation before and following foreign exploration, prompt notification concerning shipment, providing appropriate permits and relevant field notes in shipping packages, and supplying host colonies or rearing information to the quarantine laboratory.

Quarantine is a process that takes place in a specially designed, constructed, and managed area which has two goals. The first is to safely segregate intentionally imported exotic organisms from any concurrently present undesirable organisms. The second is to establish, for further use, sustainable colonies of the beneficial organisms that are the intended object of the biological control project for which the quarantine services are being performed (Fisher & Andres 1994). For a review of current and proposed USDA–ARS protocols in the United States concerning importation of exotic organisms for biological control, see Coulson & Soper (1989) and Coulson et al. (1991).

Among other things, quarantine should (1) assure that only specific beneficial organisms leave the quarantine facility, (2) coordinate the examination and identification of imported organisms with recognized taxonomic authorities, (3) provide optimal artificial environmental conditions for living exotic organisms, (4) develop the preliminary techniques to handle the exotic organisms and obtain their reproduction in the laboratory, (5) develop or review the conditions for the release of specific beneficial organisms from the quarantine facility, (6) conduct basic research on the biology and ecology of specific beneficial organisms to comply with established release criteria, and (7) maintain records of locations from which all exotic organisms have been received and to where organisms released from quarantine are sent.

Quarantine facilities are operated by the location director and quarantine officer under the terms granted by the regulating government body. In the United States this is the Animal and Plant Health Inspection Service, Plant Protection and Quarantine, within the USDA. Governing terms are contained in the certificate of approval for the quarantine laboratory. Each certificate of approval states the level of security for a specific quarantine facility. The USDA's facility in Newark, DE, for example, is "certified as sufficiently secure to confine and colonize entomophagous and phytophagous arthropods for biological control research." The certificate of approval is issued under the provisions of the Federal Plant Pest Act of 23 May 1957, and Federal Plant Pest Regulations [7 CFR 330.202(b)].

The types of organisms handled at a given facility will dictate the degree of security required. The USDA's Newark facility was designed to handle exotic parasites and predators. Other facilities have been designed to handle exotic weed-feeding insects, insect pathogens (viruses, fungi, bacteria, etc), or parasitic nematodes. The highest degree of security is required for facilities designed to process exotic plant or animal pathogens, such as the USDA's plant pathogen quarantine facility at Frederick, MD. To be certified, a quarantine facility must meet a specific set of security thresholds, given the type of organism to be processed and handled, that are required to prevent escape into the environment.

Results of biological control research conducted within the quarantine facility are used to determine whether or not a specific exotic organism can safely be released to a cooperator for additional evaluation (secondary quarantine) or for direct release into the environment. The specific information required to demonstrate safety will vary with the type of organism. For some organisms, this information may be obtained in the initial quarantine process in a short period of time. For other organisms, many months or years of testing and evaluation may be required in a variety of settings to assess the safety of the potential introduction of an agent. For all organisms it must be demonstrated that the specimens are correctly identified and free of hyperparasitism and disease. This will often require rearing the organism for one or more generations in quarantine, with examination of selected individuals for evidence of pathogens. For weed control agents, release from quarantine requires host specificity data sufficient to determine that the agent is unlikely to pose risks to crop plants or native vegetation. Most arthropods for arthropod biological control are not currently subjected to host specificity testing in the United States. Such tests are, however, routinely conducted for parasitoids that attack coccinellids or other predominantly beneficial taxa. Host specificity testing is not currently conducted to assure safety to native arthropods in the United States but may be desirable in cases where natural enemies are being introduced to regions with specialized endemic faunas.

Detailed descriptions of the structural features of quarantine laboratories that provide the physically secure environment in which the quarantine function is carried out, as well as the personnel policies that complement these architectural safeguards, are given in the next section. In the following section, methods for colonization of imported organisms in quarantine are discussed. Colonization in quarantine is required so that the organisms can be made available in sufficient numbers for study in non-quarantine laboratories and for field release. In the final section, suggestions are given as to how foreign explorers can most effectively work with the quarantine laboratory, both in terms of what materials may be shipped to the quarantine facility and with respect to providing the laboratory with host cultures and other materials or information that may be needed to colonize successfully the imported organisms.

Architectural Design and Management of Quarantine Facilities

Architectural Design. The physical layout of most quarantine facilities is similar. Differences occur relative to the size of the facility and the types of organisms to be handled. Quarantine facilities are structured around three nested layers (boxes) of confinement. The first box is the main building housing the quarantine laboratory. The second box is the quarantine laboratory itself, and the third box is made up of the individual rooms within the quarantine laboratory. For schematic drawings of some quarantine facilities see DeBach (1964) and Leppla & Ashley (1978).

The quarantine laboratory is usually constructed after the completion of the main building housing the quarantine section. This area, the "quarantine box," is completely sealed off from the nonquarantine portion of the building. Alternatively, the quarantine area may be a separate building. Within the quarantine section, each room is sealed individually from all other rooms. Each quarantine room has all the equipment, machinery, and controls necessary to set and monitor that room's environment (heating, cooling, relative humidity, photoperiod and lighting). Thus, each quarantine room can be programmed to generate and maintain a selected set of environmental conditions as needed for the specific exotic material to be processed or cultured. If a malfunction should occur in one quarantine room, the problem does not affect the environmental conditions in any other room within the quarantine area. At the USDA's Newark facility, the area above the quarantine section (referred to as the attic) is also part of the secured quarantine area and contains the water pipes, electrical conduits, and air-handling machinery. The attic area is accessible from within the quarantine area to allow personnel to perform preventive maintenance (checking filters, water condensation collection trays, electric motor belts, lubrication, etc.). A second external entrance is located in the package preparation, shipment and documentation room. This entrance is used when system repairs require the assistance of outside maintenance technicians. Major repairs by non-quarantine personnel can be accomplished without intruding on the integrity of quarantine's isolation areas.

Quarantine facilities are designed to provide adequate working space as required by the guidelines listed in facility's certificate of approval. Generally, there are four working areas: anteroom, control, preparation and isolation. The anteroom is an area outside the quarantine laboratory used to monitor the movement of personnel and materials into and out of the quarantine area. The control room is an area inside the quarantine laboratory used to prevent the escape of organisms attached to the personnel or materials leaving the quarantine area. The preparation room is an area used to hold cages, containers, and other supplies and to provide working space to prepare and clean cages or containers. This area also contains specialized storage and disposal equipment. The isolation room, farthest removed from the outside, is the space in the quarantine area where exotic organisms can be processed with the least likelihood of escape.

The physical size of a quarantine facility is dependent on funding for the construction project and the amount of space within the primary building that is allocated to the quarantine function. This will determine the number of control, preparation, and isolation rooms and other laboratory space within the quarantine area. A small quarantine facility can have as few as three rooms (control, preparation, and isolation). The USDA's Newark facility has 10 rooms: 2 anterooms (office and package preparation, and shipping and documentation), 1 control area with three cubicles, 1 preparation room, 2 laboratories for rearing and evaluation, 3 isolation rooms for natural enemy emergence and identification and 1 incoming package-handling room.

Personnel Management in Quarantine Laboratories. The potential for escape of exotic organisms exists in all quarantine facilities. The degree of risk for any given facility is largely dependent on the quality of the quarantine personnel employed to staff the facility and their adherence to quarantine procedures. Excluding major uncontrollable disasters such as earthquakes, hurricanes, tornados, and fires, escapes of quarantined organisms are most often caused by actions of careless individuals who fail to adhere to quarantine operating procedures. Such failures create opportunities for organisms to attach to clothing or materials leaving the quarantine area. To combat this potential threat of escape, all quarantine facilities have a control area where a strict set of procedures must be completed before entrance to or exit from the quarantine area is permitted. At the USDA's Frederick quarantine facility all personnel are required to shower and put on coveralls before entering the quarantine area. The same procedure is followed in reverse to exit the quarantine area. At the Newark quarantine facility, all personnel are required to wear white laboratory coats while working in the quarantine area and remove them in a designated area when leaving the quarantine area. Each part of the quarantine laboratory has a set of specific procedures which personnel entering, leaving, or carrying out activities in the area must follow.

Anteroom Procedures. Before entering the quarantine area, individuals, supplies, equipment, host plants, insects, or other materials must pass through an anteroom or inspection area. At Newark, the quarantine office and the package preparation, shipping, and documentation rooms act as the inspection area before the quarantine area is entered. All authorized personnel may take materials into the quarantine area, but only the quarantine officer or the assistant quarantine officer can remove materials, and this only after certain biological and environmental conditions and questions have been satisfied. All "first-time releases" from quarantine are reviewed by a standing committee of environmental and biological experts to guarantee that the necessary questions concerning the environmental safety of the release have been properly researched and documented.

Organism Control Room Procedures. On entering the quarantine area, the "organism control area" is encountered. This area is intended to prevent the escape of any organisms attached to clothing or bodies of personnel or materials leaving the quarantine area. The size and complexity of this area is dictated by the type of organism the facility is designed to handle. At Newark, three walk-through cubicles catch or control any organisms that may have escaped from the quarantine preparation area. The first two cubicles are dark except for light traps, which are used to attract and collect flying or crawling insects. The third cubicle contains white laboratory coats which personnel entering the quarantine area must wear. The entrance door to the preparation room has a wire-reinforced glass window to provide light which will attract insects back into the preparation room. At the Frederick quarantine facility, this area is considerably larger and equipped with locker rooms, showers, and dressing area in addition to the multiple cubicle entrance.

Preparation Room Procedures. After proceeding through the control area, one encounters the preparation room. The preparation room is generally not used to handle or process exotic organisms; it provides additional space for cage preparation and cleaning and storage of refrigerators, incubators, environmental chambers, and freezers which are used to hold exotic organisms temporarily. Refrigerators and incubators are used to store immature overwintering or diapausing organisms or adult organisms being held for authoritative identifications or shipment scheduling. The preparation area also contains a means of destroying (in an incinerator) or sterilizing (steam autoclave) discarded packaging material, host insect or plant specimens, soil, used containers, or other shipment supplies sent to the quarantine laboratory by the foreign collector.

Incoming Package Room Procedures. One room in the high-security (isolation) area of the quarantine laboratory is designated as the incoming package-handling room. This room contains all the supplies and equipment required to handle the beneficial organisms in the package properly. This room is kept cool (10–13°C) to slow the movement of organisms in the package. Under these conditions, stowaways (cockroaches, ants, or spiders, etc.) that may have crawled into the shipping container or the surrounding packing material will remain within the package while quarantine personnel remove the desired exotic beneficial organisms. All undesirable organisms and packaging materials are then placed into plastic bags (incinerator disposal) or autoclave bags (high-pressure steam sterilization). Cold temperature also slows down the activity of adult beneficial organisms. This makes it easier to place individual beneficial organisms in vials for examination and identification under the microscope. Immature stages also are examined and placed in standard emergence or overwintering containers and taken to an emergence room or placed in a refrigerator for storage.

Isolation Room Procedures. After initial examination, most immature stages of beneficial organisms contained in shipments are taken to one of the isolation rooms for later adult emergence and identification. Isolation rooms are normally set at 22°C, 60% RH, and a 16–18 h photoperiod. As the adult organisms emerge, they are placed individually in vials, examined, and identified by the quarantine officer, repackaged in a holding carton, and taken to the culture and evaluation rooms for additional biological and ecological studies or storage in refrigerators. All isolation rooms are constructed, equipped, and supplied in an identical fashion.

Laboratory Rearing Room Procedures. In most cases, exotic organisms must be reared for at least one generation within the quarantine area before they are released. This allows for identification and permits the exclusion of hyperparasitoids and pathogens. In other cases, more extended rearing may be required to exclude pathogens or to assess host preferences and range.

Quarantine personnel must devise rearing and handling procedures that permit the exotic organisms to reproduce successfully. This information is given to the foreign collector or other cooperating scientists to promote effective laboratory rearing and field release. Rearing rooms are used to perform tests intended to answer the biological and environmental questions needed to clear the organism for release from quarantine as quickly as possible. In general, parasitoids (in contrast to predators and beneficial herbivores) are not subject in their adult stage to hyperparasitism, 40–60% of all exotic parasitoid species can be released from quarantine immediately after examination and identification by the quarantine officer. These can be shipped to the cooperator or designated receiver for additional studies or direct release into the environment.

Package Preparation and Mailing Room Procedures. After the exotic organisms have been examined for any morphological deformities or abnormalities, identified by the quarantine officer (in consultation with recognized taxonomic specialists), and determined to be environmentally safe, the adults are mechanically aspirated into a shipping carton and taken to the package preparation, shipment, and documentation room. Records are createe and computerized to include all collection information, host records, and handling information for organisms received in a given shipment. The material is placed in a standard shipping package and sent to the cooperator or receiver using a 24-h commercial carrier. Upon receipt of the organism, the cooperator or receiver returns a copy of the biological shipment record, which indicates the date of arrival, the condition of the organisms, and the immediate intended use of the organisms. All documented information concerning the importation, distribution, identification, field release, deposition of designated voucher specimens, and USDA–APHIS importation permits is recorded using the incoming shipment documentation number as a reference number and is available for future use.

Procedures for Colonization in Quarantine of Imported Beneficial Species

The second function of quarantine is to colonize imported beneficial organisms in support of the biological control projects on behalf of which the importations have been made. Laboratory colonization is needed in many instances so that introduced organisms can be further screened to determine their taxonomic identity, their freedom from hyperparasitoids and pathogens, and their biological characteristics with respect to host specificity and manner of reproduction.

Colonization takes place within the isolation areas of the quarantine laboratory. To be successful, this requires sufficient physical space, controllable environment (light, temperature, relative humidity) so that conditions set are favorable to the organism at hand and, most important, a colony of the host or prey species (or plant species) needed as food by the organism to be colonized.

The exact approach taken must be tailored to the species of exotic organism being reared. Finney & Fisher (1964) and Fisher (1964) discuss, with examples, procedures for quarantine colonization. The foreign collector or other cooperating scientists can facilitate the work of the quarantine laboratory by providing whatever information is initially available on the manner of reproduction of the species, and by supplying (if needed) an initial source of the host.

In addition to facilities where the exotic organism can successfully reproduce, the quarantine laboratory will need adequate storage facilities to maintain the beneficial organisms during periods of inactivity (e.g., winter diapause) or when numbers are being accumulated to synchronize releases with field populations of the target pest.

Methods by Which the Foreign Collector May Work More Effectively with the Quarantine Laboratory

Efficient collaboration between the foreign collector and the quarantine laboratory requires that the collector understand the quarantine process, both from a scientific and legal point of view. Conversely, an effective quarantine officer must appreciate the ecological constraints that efforts to colonize an exotic natural enemy in the field are likely to impose on the scientist in charge.

To maximize the effectiveness of the collection, quarantine, and field colonization process, the collector and the quarantine officer must exchange information before, during, and after the foreign collecting trip.

Before-Trip Activities. There are four essential activities that the collector should see to before a trip: planning, permits, taxonomic support services, and a host culture to support natural enemy rearing.

Planning. Contact the quarantine officer of the facility that will be handling the material you plan to collect early in the planning phase of your project. The quarantine officer usually can provide some helpful suggestions to increase the probability of a successful shipment. The collector should provide the quarantine officer with information as to the target host, beneficial species and stages likely to be shipped, tentative collection locality, approximate number of individuals to be collected, and approximate dates of shipment. This will ensure that the quarantine facility will be expecting your material and will be prepared to receive it in terms of work load and any necessary physical preparations such as cages or host colonies.

Permits. The responsibility to obtain any required permits for the importation to quarantine of material collected at a foreign locations rests with the collector or principal scientist for the project. In the United States, APHIS–PPQ form 526, Application and Permit to Move Live Plant Pests and Noxious Weeds (Fig. 1) must be completed and approved by the appropriate state agency and USDA before any exotic material enters the country. Export permits are also required from some countries (e.g., China, Brazil, Australia). Further approvals are required before any exotic material can be shipped to the collector's laboratory (if different from the receiving facility) or approved for field release. An environmental assessment form must be completed by the applicant. Information provided is used by regulatory officials to evaluate the potential effect of release of the imported organism before issuing the permit for field release.

It is extremely important to complete the importation request accurately and early enough for the review process to occur. The quarantine officer of the facility where the field-collected material will be processed can help the collector, if necessary, with advice on how to fill out the forms. With respect to United States procedures, after completing Section A of Form 526, the collector sends the request form to the appropriate state level agency for approval, approval with conditions, or rejection. The request form then is sent to USDA–APHIS/PPQ for review and approval, sometimes with certain handling and release conditions which must be satisfied before the material can be released to the applicant. Once approved, a permit number is assigned, APHIS–PPQ labels are issued, a validity date is given and a pest category code is assigned. A copy of the final completed and signed request form and the labels are returned to the applicant, who will be responsible for sending the consignments to an approved United States quarantine laboratory for processing. Copies of permits should be included in each package sent to the quarantine facility.

Taxonomic Support Services. An essential step in clearing newly collected exotic natural enemies for field release is obtaining an authoritative identification. In some instances, these services may be routinely available through the quarantine laboratory, which may either employ taxonomists specialized in natural enemy groups or may have established relations with a national or other museum where such taxonomists are employed. It is to the collector's advantage to inquire how identifications will be obtained at the laboratory he plans to use. Such identifications, to be useful, often must be obtained rapidly. In some instances, direct prior contact with taxonomists in groups expected to be collected may be a worthwhile part of planning the collecting trip.

Host Colonies. If, as is often the case, natural enemies must be reared in quarantine for one or several generations to increase numbers before field release or to verify freedom from pathogens, it will be critical

No permit can be issued to move live plant pests or noxious weeds until an application is received (7 CFR 330 (live plant pests) or 7 CFR 360 (noxious weeds))

See reverse side for additional information

FORM APPROVED
OMB NO. 0579-0054

U.S. DEPARTMENT OF AGRICULTURE
ANIMAL AND PLANT HEALTH INSPECTION SERVICE
PLANT PROTECTION AND QUARANTINE
BIOLOGICAL ASSESSMENT AND TAXONOMIC SUPPORT
HYATTSVILLE, MARYLAND 20782

**APPLICATION AND PERMIT TO MOVE
LIVE PLANT PESTS AND NOXIOUS WEEDS**

SECTION A - TO BE COMPLETED BY THE APPLICANT

1. NAME, TITLE, AND ADDRESS (Include Zip Code)

3. TYPE OF PEST TO BE MOVED

☐ Arthropods   ☐ Noxious Weeds
☐ Pathogens   ☐ Other (Specify)

2. TELEPHONE NO.

A. SCIENTIFIC NAMES OF PESTS TO BE MOVED	B. CLASSIFICATION (Orders, Families, Races, or Strains)	C. LIFE STAGES IF APPLICABLE	D. NUMBER OF SPECIMENS OR UNITS	E. SHIPPED FROM (Country or State)	F. ARE PESTS ESTABLISHED IN U.S.	G. MAJOR HOST(S) OF THE PEST
4.						
5.						
6.						

7. WHAT HOST MATERIALS WILL ACCOMPANY WHICH PESTS (Indicate by line number)

8. DESTINATION

9. PORT OF ARRIVAL

10. APPROXIMATE DATE OF ARRIVAL OR INTERSTATE MOVEMENT

11. NO. OF SHIPMENTS

12. SUPPLIER

13. METHOD OF SHIPMENT

☐ Air Mail   ☐ Air Freight   ☐ Baggage   ☐ Auto

14. INTENDED USE (Be specific, attach outline of intended research)

15. METHODS TO BE USED TO PREVENT PLANT PEST ESCAPE

16. METHOD OF FINAL DISPOSITION

17. Applicant must be a resident of the U.S.A. I/We agree to comply with the safeguards printed on the reverse of this form, and understand that a permit may be subject to other conditions specified in Sections B and C.

SIGNATURE OF APPLICANT (Must be person named in Item 1)

18. DATE

SECTION B - TO BE COMPLETED BY STATE OFFICIAL

19. RECOMMENDATION

☐ Approve   ☐ Disapprove

☐ Accept USDA Decision

20. CONDITIONS RECOMMENDED

21. SIGNATURE

22. TITLE

STATE

23. DATE

SECTION C - TO BE COMPLETED BY FEDERAL OFFICIAL

PERMIT

24. PERMIT NO.

(Permit not valid unless signed by an authorized official of the Animal and Plant Health Inspection Service)

Under authority of the Federal Plant Pest Act of May 23, 1957 or the Federal Noxious Weed Act of 1974, permission is hereby granted to the applicant named above to move the pests described, except as deleted, subject to the conditions stated on, or attached to this application. (See standard conditions on reverse side).

This permit does not authorize the introduction, importation, interstate movement, or release into the environment of any genetically engineered organisms or products

25. SIGNATURE OF PLANT PROTECTION AND QUARANTINE OFFICIAL	26. DATE	27. LABELS ISSUED	28. VALID UNTIL	29. PEST CATEGORY

PPQ FORM 526   Previous edition may be used
(OCT 88)

Fig. 1. Application form used to regulate the importation into the United States of beneficial organisms.

that the quarantine staff working on the project have a supply of the plants, insects or other food materials that the natural enemies will require for their nourishment and reproduction. Because no quarantine laboratory can be expected to have on hand appropriate colonies for all the varied importations they may be asked to service, it is clearly an important responsibility of the collector to provide cultures of the plants, insects, or other organisms that will be needed. Considerable lead time may be needed to grow desired plants or insect colonies; this need should be addressed early in project planning in consultation with the quarantine officer of the facility that will be involved.

Activities During Exploration. During the collecting trip, the collector must be careful to ship only material specified in the importation permit, take proper collection notes, and provide notice as to dates of shipments.

What Can Be Shipped. In selecting what material and how much material is collected and shipped to quarantine, the collector should be aware of the task that quarantine staff must perform to separate the desired organisms from all other materials. In general, soil and manure should never be included in packages unless specific authorization to ship such materials has been obtained beforehand. These materials contain numerous organisms that are small and potentially dangerous. Plant material often must accompany the collected material. Nevertheless, the task of the quarantine laboratory will be made easier by keeping the quantity of plant material to the minimum needed for the importation. If the collector has knowledge that a particular shipment contains some specific contaminant which could not be excluded, specific warnings should be included in the package to alert quarantine personnel who process the shipment. In general, the shipped material should contain as little in addition to the target organism as possible to facilitate the task of the quarantine officer.

Collection Notes. Each separate shipment of foreign-collected material is potentially very different from other, seemingly similar, collections made for the same project but at different places and times. Natural enemies may differ at the species level, or populations of the same species may differ in key aspects of their biology at different locations. Contaminants may also differ greatly, both in degree and kind, between shipments. For all of these reasons, the collector must take detailed notes as to the date, location, plant species, host species, and other information as seems relevant and should include a copy of this information in each shipment so that it is immediately available to the quarantine laboratory staff. Standardized forms for collection notes are useful in this process.

Notification of Shipments. As each shipment is sent to the quarantine laboratory, contact by telephone, FAX, telex, or telegram should be made with the quarantine laboratory to advise the quarantine officer that a shipment has been made. This contact should include the shipping date, the nature and quantity of what is being shipped, when it is likely to arrive, the names and flight numbers of carrier services used, all package numbers (it may become necessary to search for lost packages), and the name of the port of entry through which the package will enter the importing country.

Post-Trip Follow-Up by the Collector. Following processing and the initial colonization in quarantine of the imported exotic organisms, the collector should remain in close contact with the quarantine staff in charge of the care and rearing of the imported species. Additional or alternative host resources may be needed if natural enemies other than those expected have been collected, or if previously provided hosts prove unacceptable to the natural enemies actually collected. A plan will be needed as to when organisms will be released from quarantine. The release process may require efforts on the part of the quarantine laboratory to store reared organisms, either to accumulate enough for release, or to synchronize natural enemy life stages with field populations of the target host.

References Cited

Coulson, J. R. & R. S. Soper. 1989. Protocols for the introduction of biological control agents in the U.S., pp. 1-35. *In* R. P. Kahn [ed.]. Plant protection and quarantine, vol. 3. Special topics. CRC, Boca Raton, Fl.

Coulson, J. R., R. S. Soper & D. W. Williams [eds.]. 1991. Biological control quarantine: needs and procedures. Appendix III. Proposed ARS guidelines for introduction and release of exotic organisms for biological control. Proceedings of a workshop USDA–ARS, ARS-99.

DeBach, P. 1964. Biological control of insects pests and weeds. Reinhold, New York.

Finney, G. L. & T. W. Fisher. 1964. Culture of entomophagous insects and their hosts, pp. 328–355. *In* P. D DeBach [ed.], Biological control of insect pests and weeds. Reinhold, New York.

Fisher, T. W. 1964. Quarantine handling of entomophagous insects, pp. 305–326. *In* P. D. DeBach [ed.], Biological control of insect pests and weeds. Reinhold, New York.

Fisher, T. W. & L. A. Andres. **1994.** Quarantine: concepts, facilities and procedures. *In* T. W. Fisher et al. [eds.], Biological control: principles and applications. University of California Press, Berkeley.

Leppla, N. C. & T. R. Ashley [eds.]. **1978.** Facilities for insect research and production. USDA Tech. Bull. 1576.

Methods for the Field Colonization of New Biological Control Agents

R. G. Van Driesche
Department of Entomology, University of Massachusetts, Amherst, MA 01003

ABSTRACT
Improvement of rates of colonization is essential to enhance effectiveness of biological control programs based on natural enemy introductions. Under ideal conditions, agents introduced should be species and strains well adapted to the target pest and able to attack it on the target crop plant. Agents should be chosen, if feasible, from sources climatically similar to intended release areas. Release areas should meet the diapause needs of agents. Release sites should be physically secure, stable, have abundant target hosts, and be well located for further spread of the agent to new areas. Numbers, quality, and stages of agents should be selected so that adequate numbers of healthy, mated (if adults), fed agents are released at colonization sites. Agents may be released in various life stages including adults, immatures, and parasitized hosts. Releases must be timed so that the life histories of the agent and target pest are appropriately synchronized. Cages and mechanical release systems must be chosen with the agent and pest biology in mind. Colonization efforts should be sustained and revised as needed until colonization is achieved or the agent is clearly shown to be biologically unable to establish. In practice, some deviation from these ideal conditions is required to prevent the loss of valuable biological material which is available at the moment.

Successful introduction of new natural enemies as a method of biological control requires the ability to establish field populations of candidate natural enemies efficiently. Only then can the potential of new agents to provide useful pest control in the new location be discovered. Historically only 34% of all attempts to colonize new agents have been successful (Hall & Ehler 1979). Failure of agents to establish can relate either to ecological factors such as interrelations of the agent's biology, the climate in the release area, or the biology of the target pest (Hagvar

1991), or to human error and technical or financial inadequacies in the introduction program (Beirne 1984). Improving the rate of establishment of introduced agents must be a major focus for biological control in the future. In this paper, methods for such improvement are presented. Matters concerning the initial choice of agents are considered first. Selection and protection of release sites are then addressed, followed by discussions of techniques for optimizing the agent (in terms of numbers, quality, and stage used for release) and of the merits of various release methods. Finally, the need for colonization efforts to be viewed as programs of activity rather than isolated events is examined.

Initial Agent Selection

In many cases, newly introduced species fail to become established because the species is not well suited for the intended purpose. For example, it may be either unable to survive the local climate or have no preference to attack the target pest. Such limitations, if known, should cause entomologists to look elsewhere for more suitable species or races of natural enemies for introduction. In practice, however, such limitations may not be apparent from information initially available about a candidate species, unless the pest/natural enemy complex has previously been studied. Although not the primary focus of this paper, it is important to briefly review the major constraints governing the selection of new natural enemies so that if the needed information is available, it can be used effectively, or if not, it can be developed early in a control program.

Is the Target Pest a Suitable Prey or Host for the Agent? Parasitoids or other types of natural enemies may be found attacking the target pest, but the association may be a weak one. Common parasitoids may, for example, occasionally attack hosts which are not their principal or preferred host or which are physiologically unsuitable for continuous reproduction of the agent. In such cases, the natural enemy may be able to reproduce for only one or two generations on the target pest. Laboratory studies may or may not be helpful in determining the suitability of the target pest for the candidate agent.

Does the Agent Attack the Target Pest Efficiently on the Target Plant? Plant characteristics such as chemical composition, leaf texture and pubescence, and plant architecture all can affect the ability of natural enemies to attack otherwise suitable hosts efficiently (Smith 1957, Monteith 1958, Elsey 1974, Smith 1978, Keller 1987, Li Zhao Hua et al. 1987). If the agent has been collected from hosts on the target plant, host plant suitability is likely assured. If, however, the target pest is found on a wide range of crop plants (e.g., *Helicoverpa armigera* [Hubner] on vegetables in Africa [van den Berg et al. 1990] or pests found in greenhouse ornamental crops), or if the pest's food plant exists in distinct varieties (e.g., hairy versus hairless varieties), or if plants from which natural enemies are collected are different from those on which the pest is to be controlled, then laboratory investigations are advisable to ensure that the agent can attack the target pest on the intended target plant. This should be accomplished before a large investment of resources is made in the colonization of one species, with the concurrent neglect of other potential candidates. For example, *Cotesia flavipes* (Cameron) populations in Pakistan preferentially seek hosts in maize over sugarcane. In contrast, an introduced population of the same species currently found in Trinidad is more attracted to hosts in sugarcane (Alam et al. 1971, Mohyuddin et al. 1981). Such plant preferences may be genetically determined, and within a single population there may exist both specialist and generalist individuals that are predisposed to recognize their hosts on only a few (or on many) plant species (Powell & Wright 1992). Such differences have important implications for successful colonization of new natural enemy species.

Is the Agent Well Adapted to the Climate in the Intended Release Area? Agents in some instances have successfully been transferred between very dissimilar climates (e.g., Bustillo & Drooz 1977). However, selection of species or races of natural enemies from areas with climates similar to that of the intended release area is a prudent approach and has been used successfully in the past (e.g., work in California for coastal versus desert areas utilizing European and Near Eastern sources of agents, respectively [Messenger et al. 1976]). Climatic factors likely to be significant are extremes of winter cold and summer heat, low relative humidities, and the effects of seasonal rainfall patterns on host and host plant availability. Climate diagrams and computerized meteorological data can be used to map similarities between regions to help direct foreign collecting to areas with appropriate climates (Sutherst & Maywald 1985, Yaninek & Bellotti 1987, Samways 1989, Maywald & Sutherst 1991). Similarly, the same information can be used to predict the likely range over which a newly introduced natural enemy (or pest) may be expected to become established. Such predictions, however, are imprecise and the limits of adaptability of new species can be known with certainty only by trial in the field.

Are the Diapause Needs of Agents Likely To Be Met in the Release Area? If agents must enter diapause to complete their seasonal cycle successfully, their diapause needs must be met in the release location if successful colonization is to be achieved. Although a number of limitations might arise, major factors include the need for an appropriate diapause host and the ability of the agent to interpret correctly the environment's diapause induction signal.

If the agent uses the target host as its diapause host, problems are unlikely to arise. If, however, another species is used that is absent in the release area, the agent may fail to establish. *Pediobius foveolatus* Crawford, for example, overwinters successfully in northern China in climates comparable to those of the northeastern United States. This race of the parasitoid, however, failed to establish in the northeast United States. It is believed that this occurred because the parasitoid overwinters in certain epilachnines (such as *Epilachna admirabilis* Crotch) which are present in Asia but absent in the United States and which overwinter as larvae. This is in contrast to the target host in the United States, the Mexican bean beetle, *Epilachna varivestis* Mulsant, which overwinters as an adult (Schaefer et al. 1983).

Correct interpretation of the environmental signals that induce diapause also can be critical because agents that enter diapause either too late or too early are unlikely to survive. For example, *Cotesia rubecula* (Marshall) from Europe failed to survive in the eastern United States (Laing & Corrigan 1987) because it entered diapause too early in the fall and had insufficient fat reserves to support itself during warm fall months (Nealis 1985). A race of *C. rubecula* imported into Massachusetts (40° N) from near Beijing, China (39° N), however, did successfully establish presumably because, among other factors, there was a favorable correspondence of the photoperiodic and climatic cycles between the collection and release locations.

Agent selection, both at the species and local population level, greatly influences the probability of successful colonization. Efficient discrimination among species and local populations will be most feasible when previously successful projects are replicated in new areas, because past experiences with the agents can be used to guide selection in projects in new areas.

Selection and Protection of Release Sites

Efforts to colonize new biological control agents can be completely frustrated if sites chosen for releases are subsequently destroyed, sprayed with pesticides, or prove to be otherwise inappropriate. Careful attention to selection of release sites and the institution of an effective management plan to preserve the sites for the time required to meet the project's goals are well worth the effort. Site characteristics that need consideration include size, security, stability, host abundance, and location.

Size. Sites should be large enough to support populations of the target pest and agent indefinitely and not be heavily influenced by pest or natural enemy movement into or out of the site. Releases of the coccinellid *Chilocorus kuwanae* (Silvestri), for example, can be made on individual infested euonymus bushes. These sites, however, may fail to support predator populations after a few months if predators reduce populations of euonymus scale, *Unaspis euonymi* (Comstock), to very low levels (personal observation). Similarly, garden-sized plots of cole crops may be too small to support populations of *Pieris rapae* L. throughout the season, in contrast to 0.25 ha or larger plots, and hence are unsuitable for the colonization of *C. rubecula.*

Security. Physical protection of release sites is crucial. Sites need to be protected from destruction, as when an orchard used for parasite releases is cut down to build houses or replanted with younger stock, and from pesticide use. This includes insecticides and miticides and may include herbicides or fungicides as well, depending on the agent being released. Greatest security is usually obtained when releases are made on property owned by the institution in charge of the project. If property owned by others is used, a written agreement is advisable if the property is owned by a business. A verbal agreement may be sufficient if the land is owned by a single individual, provided a detailed discussion is held concerning the purpose of the project and the kinds of actions that should and should not occur on or near the site. It is prudent to write a summary of the discussion and provide the cooperator with a written copy for future reference. In addition, sites should be chosen to minimize the risk of destruction from natural events, particularly flooding and fire. Discussions with the landowner or manager should reveal if a proposed site is likely to be vulnerable to such events. In some cases, the presence of dusty conditions or certain ant species may also be limiting and such sites should either be avoided or the conditions corrected before use of the site for natural enemy colonization.

Stability. Some habitats (forests, orchards, etc.) are more stable over time and in such areas past efforts to colonize new agents have been more successful than in less stable habitats such as annual crops (Greathead 1986). Stability of initial release sites for a new agent can be enhanced, however, through the development of crop management strategies in which the interests of the new agent are paramount. Ephemeral crops can be managed to enhance their stability as habitats by carefully planning dates for planting, harvest, and crop residue destruction and by establishing adjacent sequential plantings of the crop (Gilstrap 1988, Mohyuddin 1991). Harvest of the crop should not be carried out if it compromises the new agent's survival. Economics of salvaging the crop's yield should not override the goal of natural enemy establishment, otherwise the expenses incurred in the collection and rearing of the agent are wasted. If the crop must be cut or replanted to remain attractive to the target host for continued oviposition, the release plot should be large enough so that this renewal can occur in stages, with no more than one-third of the plot being removed at one time. Stability across cycles of short-season crops (e.g., cole crops in temperate areas) can be achieved by planning the entire seasonal crop cycle so that bridges are built for the natural enemy between crops both within and between seasons. *C. rubecula*, a parasitoid of *Pieris rapae* L. larvae, spins its cocoons on crop leaves and stems that are destroyed by plowing. To conserve cocoons long enough for adult parasitoids to emerge, some plots must go unplowed until new, nearby areas have been planted and become infested with young larvae of the pest. Involvement of farmers in planning for the conservation of natural enemies through such cultural practices is akin to crop rotation and can be important in providing new agents, particularly those attacking pests of row crops, with a more stable habitat. In cases where suitable prey or hosts are found on noncrop plants, these may be selected as release sites from which natural enemies can later migrate to adjacent crop fields. *Chilocorus nigritus* (F.), for example, was colonized on the nontarget scale *Asterolecanium* sp. on giant bamboo, *Dendrocalamus giganteus* Munro, in South Africa adjacent to citrus groves in which the target pest, red scale, *Aonidiella aurantii* (Maskell), occurred (Hattingh & Samways 1991).

Host Abundance and Other Foods. Sites should be selected where hosts (or prey) are known to be present in reasonable numbers. If hosts are scarce at some sites or in some years, it may be worthwhile to infest the site with the target pest. This is especially true once releases have begun at a site. The possible need to release pests at a site should be discussed in advance with the site owner. Sites should be selected, if or whenever possible, where owner permission to augment pests has been obtained. Such augmentation may be achieved either through release into sleeves or field cages, or by direct release of hosts into the crop itself. For sites at which beneficial herbivores are being colonized, manipulations may be required to enhance weed abundance or quality. For example, fertilizing *Salvinia molesta* D.S. Mitchell raised their quality as food for the weevil *Cyrtobagous* sp. and promoted its establishment (Room & Thomas 1985).

If natural enemies being released are known to require foods other than the target host or prey species, such as nectar or plant pollen, release sites should be selected or previously manipulated to provide these resources. Some phytoseiids, for example, may benefit from pollen of corn or other plants which may be established adjacent to release plots. Similarly, flowering plants can be manipulated to provide nectar and pollen for parasitoids.

Location. Sites should reflect the diversity of climatic areas where the target pest occurs. Agents released over such a range of sites can then be evaluated as to their ability to prosper and reduce the target pest in several different microclimates. In addition, the use of several sites in each zone allows each species of natural enemy in a project to be initially colonized separately. This reduces competition, which may enhance the likelihood of establishment, and provides separate locations for use as field nurseries for each species. Sites also should be selected, as far as possible, to be free of competition from previously established or native agents and their hyperparasitoids, particularly in cases where these also are able to attack the new agents. For example, hyperparasitoids of *C. glomeratus* (L.) attack *C. rubecula*, affecting the latter severely in the late season (McDonald & Kok 1992). The use of release sites with low *C. glomeratus* populations should reduce hyperparasitism of *C. rubecula* during colonization.

A final aspect of site location is the relation of the release sites to areas where crops attacked by the target pest are grown. Sites that are extremely isolated may be very favorable to initial establishment (due to protection from pesticide drift and dispersal of the agent) but may later prove too isolated to function as sources of the agent for dispersal into the broader region where the target pest must be controlled.

Optimizing the Agent: Number, Quality, and Stage

For any given species or local population of biological control agent, the probability of establishment can be affected by the number of individuals, their quality, and the life stages that are actually released.

Effect of Release Numbers. Ehler & Hall (1982) have reviewed the historical record of past attempts to colonize biological control agents. Their analysis suggests that releases of 10,000–100,000 individuals have a better chance of successful establishment (0.38–0.41) than releases of 1–10,000 individuals (0.23–0.26). Other reviews have also found a positive relationship between number released and probability of establishment (Beirne 1975, 1980). The record also contains instances where release of millions of individuals failed to result in establishment, particularly if the natural enemy was poorly adapted to the target pest (Turnbull & Chant 1961) and conversely, instances in which successful establishment has occurred from the release of <10 individuals (e.g., *Oomyzus* ("*Tetrastichus*") *incertus* (Ratzeburg) (Streams & Fuester 1967). Larger release numbers, however, do seem to aid establishment and are likely to do so in a variety of ways. At the level of the individual release site, larger numbers help maintain a larger population of the agent, counteracting dispersal and other losses in the first generation. At the project level, other influences of release number can exist. For example, if numbers of a new agent are limited, adult agents may be unavailable at critical moments (to match host availability) or releases may be limited to fewer sites and hence be less likely to include sites with features that are unrecognized but are important to natural enemy establishment. In general, thoughtful site selection, timing, and care of agents can do much to maximize the potential of small releases. Poorly timed or placed releases of large numbers of agents poor in quality are not likely to be successful because of numbers alone. If a choice between many release sites with few individuals and fewer sites with more individuals has to be made, the latter has generally been the recommended approach. Exactly how many is "too few" depends, however, on the agent. Some species establish more easily than others. The best guide is past experience with the agent.

Effect of Agent Quality. The quality of natural enemies involves genetic, health, and behavioral aspects.

Genetic Considerations. More has been written than demonstrated about how to genetically optimize new agents being colonized (see Roush 1990 for a discussion of issues involved). Suggestions have been made to either release large numbers of genetically diverse individuals from the geographic center of the agent's range and then let the new environment select out the best genotypes at the release site, or, in contrast, release agents collected from fringe populations. Such fringe populations are theorized to be less diverse because of greater selection by the source environment. These fringe populations either are or are not genetically well adapted to the release location. If they are, no further adaptation is needed and colonization is more likely. Similar conflicting advice is given as to whether to hybridize strains collected from separate locations (for increased vigor or altered host searching behaviors [Mohyuddin 1991]), or release them separately (to preserve coadapted gene complexes).

These hypotheses about the genetic consequences of various collection and release strategies have been little tested in practice. Furthermore, they pertain to the initial selection of the agent. Other genetic considerations that bear on the quality of released agents (once a source population has been chosen) include genetic drift and laboratory selection (with or without restrictions, or "bottlenecks," imposed by periodic small colony size) (Roush 1990). Drift occurs in small populations when rare alleles are lost by chance. In contrast, laboratory selection occurs in larger populations which adapt to artificial conditions over time. Laboratory selection can lead to a lowering of the quality of reared individuals used for field releases. It can be countered by release of adult agents collected as immatures in the field and reared in the laboratory only to the adult stage, thus limiting the opportunity for laboratory selection to occur. (Note that some laboratory rearing is usually needed to ensure that agents are free of disease and hyperparasitoids). This approach is feasible only if substantial numbers of immature agents (e.g., parasitized hosts) can be field-collected. Often the risk of laboratory selection must be ignored because only a few individuals can be collected in the field and the species must be reared to increase its numbers before it is released in the field. Bottlenecks in a laboratory culture occur when, regardless of the size of the founding population, the laboratory colony is temporarily reduced to a very small size, with a potential corresponding reduction in genetic diversity.

Another genetic effect, less well documented than laboratory selection, is swamping of incipient field strains. This concept assumes that the released populations of the agent are rapidly selected by the release environment and become better adapted. If repeated releases of large numbers of a standard laboratory stock of the agent are made, field selection of an improved strain will be thwarted by breeding with the recently released laboratory stock. Under this scenario, releases should be as large as possible initially and then discontinued after one or two generations. The practical importance of this approach has not been demonstrated.

Health and Motivation of Agents. Adults are often the stage used to colonize new biological control agents (but also see the section on the use of immature stages). When adults are released, it is important that they be in good health, fed, mated, preexposed to the target host, and handled with care during transport to the release site. In general, adults should be released within a few days (2–5) of emergence because the oviposition capacity of many agents, especially some parasitoids, reaches a maximum early in adult life. Adults should be well cared for during the time between emergence and release in the field. Most important, they must be supplied with food and water and not exposed to damaging temperatures or condensation. Honey is a commonly used artificial food source for parasitoids, although for some species access to sources of protein (host fluids or bird excrement) may also be needed. For predators, access to prey, honey, pollen, fungal spores, or other foods may be needed. Herbivores may require opportunities to feed on the target plant in an appropriate growth stage. Some organisms may also need a source of free water. For small parasitoids, thick honey deposits and condensation can themselves cause mortality, and appropriate choices of cage or container materials and temperatures must be made to prevent such losses.

Agents must also be free of disease and hyperparasitoids. These should initially be screened out by quarantine, but pathogens or hyperparasitoids may invade laboratory cultures if individuals collected in the field (in the areas of introduction) are added to the colony (e.g., Geden et al. 1992). Continued monitoring of reared agents is important to guard against these problems.

Adult agents must also be mated to ensure a suitable sex ratio among offspring. Some species may mate without special environmental conditions. Others may require specific lighting, cage dimensions, or other conditions. Some parasitoids, for example, require exposure to natural sunlight. This can be provided by placing cages of adults outdoors or in rooms with direct natural sunlight soon after emergence. Such cages should also include the plant and target host in the suitable stage for oviposition. Some tachinids may mate more readily in larger cages and may require natural light. With new species it is advisable to observe adults directly to detect mating to assure that rearing conditions are suitable. Failure to obtain a high frequency of mating among females in a culture also may arise from an unfavorable sex ratio. This may result from poor conditions for mating in the previous generation, small hosts, or other factors.

Studies on learning in insects (Lewis & Tumlinson 1988, Carde & Hai-poong Lee 1989, Wardle & Borden 1989) suggest that performance of some natural enemies such as hymenopteran parasitoids can be improved by exposing newly emerged adults to the target host on the target plant and allowing them to oviposit before they are released. Frass or plant-derived materials often contain important stimuli that affect natural enemy foraging behavior (e.g., van Leerdam et al. 1985, Nealis 1986, Auger et al. 1989, Shu et al. 1990). Contact with these materials may also increase the likelihood that parasitoids will immediately search for hosts once released rather than dispersing. Such exposure is particularly important if rearing conditions are highly artificial or involve the use of a rearing host or prey different than the target species.

Finally, adults must be protected from adverse conditions during transport to the release sites. The use of coolers to guard against overheating is essential. If shipping requires >1 d, food must be provided and precautions taken against damaging temperatures by shipping in insulated containers.

Effect of Life Stage of Agent Used for Release. Releases of biological control agents consist most commonly of adults but may in some cases include immature stages (often pupae or cocoons) or parasitized hosts (Moorehead & Maltby 1970, Dysart et al. 1973, USDA 1978, Hattingh & Samways 1991). Adults are often preferred because released individuals are ready to reproduce and will be less exposed to predation and other mortality factors before reproduction begins. However, adults may be a less durable stage and may suffer losses enroute to the release locations (if shipment is required) or may disperse over such large areas that their offspring cannot find each other to mate.

Eggs (for predators and weed-feeding herbivores) or pupae (for parasitoids) are sometimes used as a release stage. Advantages of the use of these stages are that they are durable, do not require food or water, and are easy to transport or ship. In addition, the use of pupae allows adults to emerge in their natural habitat, which is likely to have a positive effect on their subsequent behavior, limiting dispersal. However, eggs or pupae may suffer losses from predators or hyperparasitoids and newly emerged adults may have difficulty locating each other to mate. This latter problem should be minimal if cocoons are placed in natural locations and deployed in densities normally found in field populations.

For parasitoids, a third choice of stage for release is the immature stage(s) in or on parasitized hosts. In some cases, parasitized hosts can be collected in large numbers and moved to new sites. Dysart et al. (1973) describes the successful mass collection at field sites of larvae of cereal leaf beetle, *Oulema melanopus* (L.), parasitized by *Tetrastichus julis* (Walker) and their movement to new locations. In a similar manner, numerous releases have been made using parasitized alfalfa weevil larvae and tarnished plant bug nymphs collected by sweeping in fields where the desired parasitoids were established and hosts were still abundant. This process lends itself to use by farmers and extension or government personnel in large regional redistribution programs (e.g., USDA 1978). (Some concerns about spreading pests or diseases may exist and should be carefully considered before undertaking such a program.) Release of parasitized stages rather than adult parasitoids is especially useful if adults are delicate or short-lived (e.g., mymarids such as *Anaphes flavipes* (Foerster), which was released by placing containers of parasitized host eggs in the field [Moorehead & Maltby 1970, Maltby et al. 1971]. Release of immature parasitoids in parasitized hosts also allows at least some types of adelphoparasitism (those in which males develop as parasitoids of conspecific females) to be dealt with effectively. By placing plants bearing parasitized hosts of a range of ages (as for example certain whiteflies and their parasitoids [e.g., Sailer et al. 1984]) in the field, entire colonies can be transferred. This places a staggered set of host and immature parasitoid stages at the site and ensures that hosts bearing immature female parasitoids will be present to serve as hosts for male progeny. One disadvantage of the use of parasitized hosts as the release stage is that there may be losses to predators, hyperparasitoids, and other factors before released individuals have an opportunity to reproduce.

Optimizing Release Methods

Once the choices have been made of which agent will be released, of what quality and stage, and at what sites, the release itself occurs. Timing the release so that the appropriate agent and target host life stages are brought together is crucial if the agent is to reproduce. For some target pests, such as some scales in which the stages used as prey or hosts are present over long periods of time (e.g., release of adult *C. kuwanae*, which can feed on several scale stages including eggs, adult females, and larger nymphs) (personal observation), timing is not an issue. For other species it can be critical. Releases of *C. rubecula*, for example, must be timed so that adult wasps are present when first- or second-instar *P. rapae* larvae are present (Yang 1985, & personal observation). Release of adult *Holcothorax testaceipes* (Ratzeburg), an encyrtid parasite of the apple blotch leafminer, *Phyllonorycter crataegella* Clemens), must coincide with the presence of host eggs (Sekita & Yamada 1979, personal observation). If adult parasitoids are the released stage and if the target pest stage is readily visible, whether a given site is ready for a release can be determined by sampling on or just before the date of the intended release. If, on the other hand, the target stage is scarce, tiny, or embedded in plant tissue, it may be very difficult to assess its presence (e.g., eggs of *P. crataegella*, the host of *H. testaceipes*, are too small and scarce to be used readily to time releases). In such cases it may be possible to forecast dates for releases from samples of earlier stages. The occurrence of *P. crataegella* eggs, for example, can be predicted by using colored sticky traps to monitor the presence of adult moths, knowing that eggs will follow within a few days. If cocoons or pupae rather than adult parasitoids are the stages to be released, a further estimate will be needed as to how much time will pass before adult parasitoids emerge.

The simultaneous release of several stages (adults, cocoons, parasitized hosts) will prolong the period over which the agent is present in the adult stage, promoting increased synchrony with the target host stage. This strategy may be especially useful in cases in which host recruitment into the target stage occurs over a long period or is hard to detect.

Other than timing to assure synchrony of the target pest and the released agent, the aspect of release methodology that most commonly requires some decision is whether to place agents initially into field cages (or sleeve cages) stocked with hosts or to release the agents freely onto plants. Cages allow one or more cycles of reproduction by the agent in an environment in which host abundance is assured, agent dispersal is restricted, and competitors (such as other parasitoids and predators) are excluded. *H. testaceipes* releases, for example, benefit from such an approach because in unsprayed apple plots in the northeastern United States, another parasitoid, *Sympiesis marylandensis* Girault, is very common. This parasitoid acts after *H. testaceipes* and because it is an external parasitoid (in contrast to *H. testaceipes* which is an internal parasitoid), *H. testaceipes* immatures are killed if their host is attacked by *S. marylandensis*. This loss can be avoided during initial *H. testaceipes* releases if sleeve cages, stocked with adult leafminers, are used and left in place until after hosts parasitized by *H. testaceipes* are too mature for attack by *S. marylandensis* (unpublished data). This occurs once *H. testaceipes* begins to pupate in their hosts. Cages can then be removed in time to allow the free emergence of the new *H. testaceipes* adults.

Cages can, however, cause problems. If they became too hot, too wet, or otherwise unsuitable, agents are unable to move to a better area and may die. Agents are confined to the cage and so cannot search elsewhere if hosts are too scarce, or are less than optimal in stage or quality or if some resource (e.g., honeydew) is lacking. Finally, some agents simply do not mate and reproduce well in small cages.

The advantages of using cages must be assessed for each agent. Initially it may be prudent to use several methods simultaneously, placing some of the available agents at a release site in cages and releasing others directly into the field. This approach was used to establish the Chinese strain of *C. rubecula* in Massachusetts, in which only 150 adults (reared from parasitized larvae from China) were initially available (unpublished data). Most of these adults were placed in stocked field cages to multiply their numbers. Others were released directly into the field. This approach was repeated three times, and after each cycle of reproduction in field cages a portion of the resulting adults and cocoons were released and others were retained in field cages.

Other aspects of release technology of interest are selection of time of day for release and systems for mechanical release, sometimes by air, to cover large areas.

If adult agents of species that fly readily are released, and if no cages are to be used, it may be best to make releases in the early morning because lower light intensity and cooler temperatures are less likely to cause agents to fly out of the release plot immediately. Warming will occur slowly as the day progresses, allowing agents to become adjusted to their new location gradually, encounter hosts, and become oriented to host-seeking rather than dispersal. If nonadult stages are released, the time of day for the release is of less importance.

Mechanical release systems may be developed for projects whose size dictates a need for methods to speed up the release process and to make it possible to place agents in plots rapidly with little or no assessment of the circumstances in the plot. This is often done by air (e.g., Pickett et al. 1987). In undeveloped regions where roads are lacking, aerial releases may be the only feasible approach. *Epidinocarsis lopezi* DeSantis, for example, was released successfully in tropical Africa from airplanes by dropping vials containing adult wasps, which were able to escape after vials reached the ground (Herren et al. 1987). The method worked because host abundance was high throughout the treated areas, the parasitoid could attack all of its host's life stages (except egg and adult males), and no host/parasitoid synchrony problems existed. A technique to disperse phytoseiids by air using vials with strings (which catch on crop plants and provide crawling routes for the phytoseiids from vials to foliage) has also been developed for use in the same areas of tropical Africa (Herren et al. 1987). Aerial dispersal may also be used effectively to redistribute agents that are effective locally but disperse slowly. The encyrtid *Neodusmetia sangwani* (Rao), for example, was distributed by the use of aircraft over large areas in Texas to control the Rhodesgrass mealybug, *Antonina graminis* (Maskell) (Schuster et al. 1971).

Planning Colonization Programs

The colonization of a new agent, like many endeavors, may require repeated attempts before success is achieved or failure can safely be attributed to biological inadequacy of the agent. The time required for colonization programs will vary and should not be limited to arbitrarily defined periods (e.g., the "three year rule" sometimes mentioned in biological control programs). Colonization should be viewed as a program, not as a one-time event. Three important features of colonization programs are monitoring, reserves, and documentation.

Monitoring implies the need for continuing review of the progress of a release. Have site conditions changed? Did a certain approach work? If not, why not? Assessment of results must continue for as long as needed to achieve success. One of the most common failures in technique which cause colonization attempts to fail is that the efforts made are too few, with no reassessment and further action. Agents are liberated and nothing more is done. This "sink or swim" approach is very detrimental to success. Entomologists should undertake the colonization of new agents only if they have the commitment and resources to follow through as needed. Entomologists should actively seek to understand what difficulties the incipient population of the new agent will face and do everything possible to reduce or mitigate these problems. The population of the agent should not be expected to be robust during the colonization phase. Small numbers of an agent population make it more vulnerable to adversities than after it has become more numerous and widespread. Entomologists should actively seek to intervene on behalf of populations in the process of colonization. If hosts are too scarce, more should be added if possible. If special arrangements are needed to maintain and protect the habitat from destruction such as harvesting, plowing, burning, or mowing, they should be made. If additional releases are needed to reenforce the population of an agent at a site where problems have occurred, such recolonization efforts should be made by taking agents from a laboratory colony or from another field site.

Reserves for releases require access to populations of the agent from which individuals for additional releases may be taken. This may be a laboratory colony of the agent or field plots that can serve as nurseries from which the agent can be collected. Laboratory colonies have an advantage in that some agents can be reared to a storable life stage and accumulated for later release. In this way many months of rearing production can be available for releases in a short "window of opportunity" when hosts are in appropriate life stages, or very early in the season so that more time is available for the agent to increase its numbers. If field-collected organisms are used for redistribution, they should be reviewed carefully so that hyperparasitoids or diseases attacking the agent at field nurseries are not spread to new locations.

Documentation of all releases and recoveries efforts made in a colonization program is an essential part of the process. Careful records should be kept of the dates and locations of all releases, the physical and biological conditions at each site, and the numbers and stages of agents released. Dates of each postrelease monitoring collection should be noted, along with the observed levels of the agent. This information is essential to guide release programs and for eventual publication of program results. In addition, information concerning releases should be submitted to state and national agencies responsible for the maintenance of information on biological control efforts for incorporation into appropriate data bases, as for example that maintained in the United States by USDA-ARS (ROBO, Releases of Beneficial Organisms in the United States and Territories) (Coulson 1992). Inclusion of such data in international data bases, such as that on world releases of arthropods for control of arthropods maintained by IIBC in the United Kingdom and on releases of arthropods for control of weeds maintained by CSIRO in Australia, is also valuable.

Conclusion

Colonization of new natural enemies is a critical step in the use of importation for biological pest control. Success in colonization can be increased through a number of actions, beginning with the choice of appropriate agents, the careful selection and maintenance of release sites, and the liberation of numerous, healthy specimens of the agent with techniques designed to favor their survival and reproduction. The process of establishing natural enemies requires thoughtful, persistent attention from biologists familiar with the agent and its target host. Efforts made with attention to detail will be most likely to succeed.

References Cited

Alam, M. M., F. D. Bennett & K. P. Carl. 1971. Biological control of *Diatraea saccharalis* (F.) in Barbados by *Apanteles flavipes* Cam. and *Lixophaga diatraeae* T.T. Entomophaga 16: 151-158.

Auger, J., C. LeComte, J. Paris & E. Thibout. 1989. Identification of leek-moth and diamondback-moth Frays volatiles that stimulate parasitoid, *Diadromus pulchellus*. J. Chem. Ecol. 15: 1391-1398.

Beirne, B. P. 1975. Influences on the development and evolution of biological control in Canada. Bull. Entomol. Soc. Can. 5: 85-89.

1980. Biological control: benefits and opportunities, pp. 307-321. *In* Anonymous [ed.], Perspectives in world agriculture. Commonwealth Agriculture Bureaux, Farnharm, U.K.

1984. Avoidable obstacles to colonization in classical biological control of insects. Can. J. Zool. 63: 743-747.

Bustillo, A. E. & A. T. Drooz. 1977. Cooperative establishment of a Virginia (USA) strain of *Telenomus alsophilae* on *Oxydia trychiata* in Colombia. J. Econ. Entomol. 70: 767-770.

Carde, R. T. & Hai-poong Lee. 1989. Effect of experience on the responses of the parasitoid *Brachymeria intermedia* (Hymenoptera: Chalcididae) to its host *Lymantria dispar* (Lepidoptera: Lymantriidae), and to kairomone. Ann. Entomol. Soc. Am. 82: 653-657.

Coulson, J. R. 1992. Documentation of classical biological control introductions. Crop Prot. 11: 195-205.

Dysart, R. J., H. L. Maltby & M. H. Brunson. 1973. Larval parasites of *Oulema melanopus* in Europe and their colonization in the United States. Entomophaga 18: 133-167.

Ehler, L. E. & R. W. Hall. 1982. Evidence for competitive exclusion of introduced natural enemies in biological control. Environ. Entomol. 11: 1-4.

Elsey, K. D. 1974. Influence of plant host on searching speed of two predators. Entomophaga 19: 3-6.

Geden, C. J., L. Smith, S. J. Long & D. A. Rutz. 1992. Rapid deterioration of searching behavior, host destruction and fecundity of the parasitoid *Muscidifurax raptor* (Hymenoptera: Pteromalidae) in culture. Ann. Entomol. Soc. Am. 85: 179-187.

Gilstrap, F. E. 1988. Sorghum-corn-Johnsongrass and Banks grass mite: a model for biological control in field crops, pp. 141-158. *In* M.K. Harris & C.E. Rogers [eds.], The entomology of indigenous and naturalized systems in agriculture. Westview, Boulder, CO.

Greathead, D. J. 1986. Parasitoids in classical biological control, pp. 289-315. *In* J. Waage & D. Greathead [eds.], Insect parasitoids. Academic, London.

Hagvar, E. B. 1991. Ecological problems in the establishment of introduced predators and parasites for biological control. Acta Entomol. Bohemoslov. 88: 1-11.

Hall, R. W. & L. E. Ehler. 1979. Rate of establishment of natural enemies in classical biological control. Bull. Entomol. Soc. Am. 25: 280-282.

Hattingh, V. & M. J. Samways. 1991. Determination of the most effective method for field establishment of biocontrol agents of the genus *Chilocorus* (Coleoptera: Coccinellidae). Bull. Entomol. Res. 81: 169-174.

Herren, H. R., T. J. Bird & D. J. Nadel. 1987. Technology for automated aerial release of natural enemies of the cassava mealybug and cassava green mite. Insect Sci. Applic. 8: 883-885.

Keller, M. A. 1987. Influence of leaf surface on movements by the hymenopterous parasitoid *Trichogramma exiguum*. Entomol. Exp. Appl. 43: 55-59.

Laing, J. E. & J. E. Corrigan. 1987. Intrinsic competition between the gregarious parasite *Cotesia glomeratus* and the solitary parasite *Cotesia rubecula* (Hymenoptera: Braconidae) for their host *Artogeia rapae* (Lepidoptera: Pieridae). Environ. Entomol. 32: 493-501.

Lewis, W. J. & J. H. Tumlinson 1988. Host detection by chemically mediated associative learning in a parasitic wasp. Nature 331(6153): 257-259.

Li Zhao Hua, F. Lamnes, J. C. van Lenteren, P. W. T. Huisman, A. van Vianen & O. M. B. de Ponti. 1987. The parasite-host relationship between *Encarsia formosa* Gahan (Hymenoptera, Aphelinidae) and *Trialeurodes vaporariorum* (Westwood) (Homoptera, Aleyrodidae). XXV. Influence of leaf structure on the searching activity of *Encarsia formosa*. J. Appl. Entomol. 104: 297-304.

Maltby, H. L., F. W. Stehr, R. C. Anderson, G. E. Moorehead, L. C. Barton & J. D. Paschke. 1971. Establishment in the United States of *Anaphes flavipes*, an egg parasite of the cereal leaf beetle. J. Econ. Entomol. 64: 693-697.

Maywald, G. F. & R. W. Sutherst. 1991. User's guide to CLIMEX. A computer program for comparing climates in ecology, 2nd ed. CSIRO Div. Entomol. Rep. 35.

McDonald, R. C. & L. T. Kok. 1992. Colonization and hyperparasitism of *Cotesia rubecula* (Hymen.: Braconidae), a newly introduced parasite of *Pieris rapae*, in Virginia. Entomophaga 37: 223-228.

Messenger, P. S., E. Biliotti & R. van den Bosch. 1976. The importance of natural enemies in integrated control, pp. 543-563. *In* C. B. Huffaker & P.S. Messenger [eds.], Theory and practice of biological control. Academic, New York.

Mohyuddin, A. I. 1991. Utilization of natural enemies for the control of insects pests of sugar-cane. Insect Sci. Applic. 12: 19-26.

Mohyuddin, A. I., C. Inayatullah & E. G. King. 1981. Host selection and strain occurrence in *Apanteles flavipes* (Cameron) (Hymenoptera: Braconidae) and its bearing on biological control of graminaceous stem-borers (Lepidoptera: Pyralidae). Bull Entomol. Res. 71: 575-581.

Monteith, L. G. 1958. Influence of food plant of host on attractiveness of the host to tachinid parasites with notes on preimaginal conditioning. Can. Entomol. 90: 478-482.

Moorehead, G. E. & H. L. Maltby. 1970. A container for releasing *Anaphes flavipes* from parasitized eggs of *Oulema melanopus*. J. Econ. Entomol. 63: 675-676.

Nealis, V. 1985. Diapause and the seasonal ecology of the introduced parasite *Cotesia* (*Apanteles*) *rubecula* (Hymenoptera: Braconidae). Can. Entomol. 117: 333-342.

  1986. Responses to host kairomones and foraging behavior of the insect parasite *Cotesia rubecula* (Hymenoptera: Braconidae). Can. J. Zool. 64: 2393-2398.

Pickett, C. H., F. E. Gilstrap, R. K. Morrison & L. F. Bouse. 1987. Release of predatory mites (Acari: Phytoseiidae) by aircraft for the biological control of spider mites (Acari: Tetranychidae) infesting corn. J. Econ. Entomol. 80: 906-910.

Powell, W. & A. F. Wright. 1992 (typographical error in original, actually 1991). The influence of host food plants on host recognition of four aphidiine parasitoids (Hymenoptera: Braconidae). Bull. Entomol. Res. 81: 449-453.

Room, P. M. & P. A. Thomas. 1985. Nitrogen and establishment of a beetle for biological control of the floating weed *Salvinia* in Papua New Guinea. J. Appl. Ecol. 22: 139-156.

Roush, R. T. 1990. Genetic variation in natural enemies: critical issues for colonization in biological control, pp. 263-288. *In* M. Mackauer, L. Ehler & J. Roland [eds.], Critical issues in biological control. Intercept, Andover, U.K.

Sailer, R. I., R. E. Brown, B. Mumir & J. C. E. Nickerson. 1984. Dissemination of the citrus whitefly (Homoptera: Aleyrodidae) parasitoid *Encarsia lahorensis* (Howard) (Hymenoptera: Aphelinidae) and its effectiveness as a control agent in Florida. Bull. Entomol. Soc. Am. 30: 36-39.

Samways, M. J. 1989. Climate diagrams and biological control: an example from the areography of the ladybird *Chilocorus nigritus* (Fabricius, 1798) (Insecta, Coleoptera, Coccinellidae). J. Biogeogr. 16: 345-351.

Schaefer, P. W., R. J. Dysart, R. V. Flanders, T. L. Burger & K. Ikebe. 1983. Mexican bean beetle (Coleoptera: Coccinellidae) larval parasite *Pediobius foveolatus* (Hymenoptera: Eulophidae) from Japan: field release in the United States. Environ. Entomol. 12: 852-854.

Schuster, M. F., J. C. Boling & J. J. Morony, Jr. 1971. Biological control of rhodesgrass scale by airplane releases of an introduced parasite of limited dispersing ability, pp. 227-250. *In* C.B. Huffaker [ed.], Biological control. Plenum, New York.

Sekita, N. & M. Yamada. 1979. Studies on the population of the apple leaf miner *Phyllonorycter ringoniella* Matsumura (Lepidoptera: Lithocolletidae) III. Some analyses of the mortality factors operating upon the population. Appl. Entomol. Zool. 14: 137-148.

Shu, S., P. D. Swedenborg & R. L. Jones. 1990. A kairomone for *Trichogramma nubilale* (Hymenoptera: Trichogrammatidae) isolation, identification and synthesis. J. Chem. Ecol. 16: 521-529.

Smith, D. A. S. 1978. Cardiac glycosides in *Canaus chrysippus* (L.) provide some protection against an insect parasitoid. Experientia 34: 844-845.

Smith, J. M. 1957. Effects of the food plant of California red scale, *Aonidiella aurantii* (Masko) on reproduction of its hymenopterous parasites. Can. Entomol. 89: 219-230.

Streams, F. A. & R. W. Fuester. 1967. Biology and distribution of *Tetrastichus incertus*, a parasite of the alfalfa weevil. J. Econ. Entomol. 60: 1574-1579.

Sutherst, R. W. & G. F. Maywald. 1985. A computerized system for matching climates in ecology. Agric. Ecosyst. Eviron. 13: 281-299.

Turnbull, A. L. & D. A. Chant. 1961. The practice and theory of biological control of insects in Canada. Can. J. Zool. 39: 694-744.

USDA. 1978. Nonchemical control of the cereal leaf beetle. USDA APHIS Picture Story 309.

van den Berg, H., B. T. Nyambo & J. K. Waage. 1990. Parasitism of *Helicoverpa armigera* (Lepidoptera: Noctuidae) in Tanzania: analysis of parasitoid-crop associations. Environ. Entomol. 70: 767-770.

van Leerdam, M. B., J. W. Smith, Jr. & T. W. Fuchs. 1985. Frass-mediated, host-finding behavior of *Cotesia flavipes*, a braconid parasite of *Diatraea saccharalis* (Lepidoptera: Pyralidae). Ann. Entomol. Soc. Am. 78: 647-650.

Wardle, A. R. & J. H. Borden. 1989. Learning of an olfactory stimulus associated with a host microhabitat by *Eristes roborator*. Entomol. Exp. Appl. 52: 271-279.

Yang, H. W. 1985. Bionomics of *Apanteles rubecula* Marshall. Chinese Journal of Biological Control 1: 6-10 (in Chinese).

Yaninek, J. S. & A. C. Bellotti. 1987. Exploration for natural enemies of cassava green mites based on agrometeorological criteria, pp. 69-75. *In* D. Rijks & G. Mathys [eds.], Proceedings of the seminar on agrometeorology and crop protection in the lowland humid and sub-humid tropics, Cotonou, Benin, 7-11 July 1986. World Meteorological Organization, Geneva.

Conclusions

R. G. Van Driesche
Department of Entomology, University of Massachusetts, Amherst, MA 01003

T. S. Bellows, Jr.
Department of Entomology, University of California, Riverside, CA 92521

Although many conclusions and recommendations might be drawn from the preceding discussions of the various steps in classical biological control, several key ideas deserve emphasis.

First, state or national level programs of biological control, to be effective, must be adequately financed. Biological control is not cheap. Because significant sums of money, once dedicated to particular projects, will not be available for other possible biological control uses, it is important that good selections of target pests be made. Making good judgments as to which pest problems are most likely to be successfully resolved through biological control, and of these, which are sufficiently serious, economically or ecologically, that they need to be resolved, is likely to require careful gathering of extensive information. Every effort should be made to avoid work on species that have a low probability, in view of their biological characteristics, of being successfully suppressed and to avoid work on projects in which losses do not substantially exceed the cost of conducting biological control. Making appropriate target selections will require that extensive, often obscure, scientific literature and museum records be obtained and synthesized, and that this information be subjected to analysis based on well-reasoned arguments and the experience of scientists who have successfully conducted projects of classical biological control in the past.

The foreign exploration, shipping, and quarantine processes that are basic to classical biological control need extensive logistical support of a sustained nature. Taxonomic support is especially important because correct identifications of pests and their natural enemies are absolutely essential for effective biological control. Success in these activities is nearly always proportional to the effort made. Fragmented, insufficiently broad, or prematurely terminated searches are unlikely to be successful and may even convey the erroneous impression that effective natural enemies do not exist. Governmental institutions need to recognize the special needs of this type of work and programs should be designed to facilitate and support the work over time frames appropriate to the task.

Finally, it should be emphasized how important the skill of establishing new natural enemies is to all of classical biological control. Comprehensive, sustained efforts are needed to create environments that are favorable to the establishment of the natural enemies which are released. The economic value of the natural enemy germplasm collected through foreign exploration is high, and its potential should be conserved by use of the most effective establishment methods available. Specific research on methods to improve establishment might be a future area of emphasis for biological control agencies.

Renewal of biological control institutions and vigorous application of the method are needed to resolve arthropod pest control problems an environmentally responsible manner.